"WHAT DEGREE OF MADNESS?"

"WHAT DEGREE OF MADNESS?"
Madison's Method to Make America STATES Again

JOE A. WOLVERTON, II, J.D.

FOREWORD BY MICHAEL BOLDIN
Founder and Executive Director of the Tenth Amendment Center

SHOTWELL PUBLISHING
Columbia, South Carolina

Produced in the Republic of South Carolina by

SHOTWELL PUBLISHING, LLC
Post Office Box 2592
Columbia, South Carolina 29202

www.ShotwellPublishing.com

Cover Design: Hailey Galloway

ISBN: 978-1-947660-30-4

10 9 8 7 6 5 4 3 2 1

Joe Wolverton's latest book provides a message America needs. America needs a course correction. Instead of following the success formula set forth in our founding documents, The Declaration of Independence and The Constitution, we have been traveling a suboptimal path. Restoration of the proper relationship between the states and the federal government will restore the greatest freedom to our country. We will no longer have a national government but will bring us back to a federal government which will bring lasting freedom and prosperity. Joe's scholarship and writing on this important topic is vital to our nation's future.

— Rep. Andy Biggs (R-Ariz.)

"State nullification" has always been part of the American political tradition, but since the Civil War a largely suppressed part. Today, however, state nullification (and even secession) are again topical—though not well understood. This book—well suited for a general audience—is a thorough study of the importance of state nullification today as a lawful instrument for resisting federal tyranny.

— Donald Livingston, Prof. of Philosophy, Emory University (retired) and President, Abbeville Institute

Joe Wolverton gets to the heart of the fundamental problem in American society: aggressive nationalism. His prescription for making "STATES again" is nothing short of fantastic. Anyone who believes we need to be "thinking locally and acting locally" needs to read this book.

— Dr. Brion McClanahan, author of *9 Presidents Who Screwed Up America, How Alexander Hamilton Screwed Up America*, and many other titles

The U.S. government was created as the joint agent of the peoples of sovereign States. It was designed to manage those interests that the States shared and it was of specifically limited powers. No honest observer can deny this historical truth. Today we have a federal government that has no limits on its power—that controls toilets and parking lots and has a hundred military installations around the world. While the States are nearly inert. But the States are what we have. They are historical realities and potential points of power and allegiance. Joe Wolverton, a prolifically published constitutional lawyer, shows how the States might become restrainers of illegal federal acts. What other hope do we have against Leviathan?

— Clyde N. Wilson, Emeritus Distinguished Professor of History, University of South Carolina.

To my wife, Kylee.
There has never been a more exemplary Southern woman,
which says a lot for someone from Burley, Idaho.

To Donald Robertson:
James Madison's teacher, my teacher, and a proud patriot.
May you and Mr. Madison be pleased with my work.

Contents

Foreword

WE THE PEOPLE.

You've undoubtedly heard these words at one time or another.

But it's not just a flowery phrase to rally support for a politician or a cause. It's truly the foundation of something that was entirely new when the Constitution's framers presented the document for ratification in 1787.

Writing in support of ratification to "the People of the State of New York," James Madison emphasized the importance of this phrase in *Federalist* No. 46.

"The federal and State governments are in fact but different agents and trustees of the people, constituted with different powers, and designed for different purposes," Madison wrote, reminding readers that the "ultimate authority ... resides in the people alone."

But yet, there was significant opposition to ratification; and in few places was that opposition as strong as in New York.

One of the greatest concerns from the opposition was that of "consolidation," or centralization of power.

In Pennsylvania, Tench Coxe sought to address these concerns when he wrote, "The thirteen United States were not intended to be, and really are not consolidated, in such manner as to absorb or destroy the sovereignties of the several states."

And in New York, Madison worked to do the same with *Federalist* No. 46, pointing out that should the federal government engage in an "unwarrantable" measure (read: unconstitutional), or even an unpopular "warrantable" (constitutional) one, "the means of opposition to it are powerful and at hand."

Notably absent from Madison's powerful ways to oppose a federal act are those which most people attempt today. Instead, Madison recommended a series of actions to be taken at the state and individual level, noting that should several "adjoining States" take the same stand, it "would present obstructions which the federal government would hardly be willing to encounter."

Unfortunately, however, these are not common topics in government schools, on the campaign stump, or in most political commentary. And that is just one of many reasons why it's so important to read and share this book.

—Michael Boldin

Founder & Executive Director of the Tenth Amendment Center

Chapter 1

The Gathering Storm

THE UNITED STATES is being divided again by a second civil war. So far, this crisis is a cold war, but the threat of armed revolution is growing as citizens and state legislators fight for beachheads of sovereignty against the immensely stronger (and more well-armed) forces of the federal government.

The agents of the so-called federal government are aware, though, that they have the states at a materiel disadvantage.

In November 2018, after being told that his attempt to confiscate "assault rifles" from Americans would result in a war, Representative Eric Swalwell (D-Calif.) predicted a quick end to such a showdown over the Second Amendment.

"And it would be a short war my friend. The government has nukes. Too many of them," Swalwell tweeted.

The United States has certainly turned a corner toward total armed civil strife when a sitting member of Congress threatens (sarcastically, he claimed) to use the federal government's nuclear arsenal to quell any attempt by citizens to keep and bear arms in the face of federal forces tasked with taking them away.

For the present, though, several states have already fired on federal troops — not with bullets, but with bills. Every day resolutions are filed in state houses, declaring federal acts masked as laws: "null, void, and of no legal effect." The constitutionally offensive federal acts most often targeted by state lawmakers in recent years are: Obamacare, the National Defense Authorization Act (NDAA), the constant surveillance by the National Security Agency (NSA) and several other federal departments, and the abrogation of the right to keep and bear arms as protected by the Second Amendment. To date, only a few courageous state representatives have enlisted in the battalions set to battle Washington, D.C., defy its mandates, and lay down cover fire for the all-volunteer movement marching toward recovery of the Constitution. As yet, this is a bloodless revolution.

It's my hope and my purpose for writing this book to reveal a constitutionally sound solution to the struggle between those working to restore state sovereignty and those working to increase the size of the American empire. The answer should sound a little familiar: Make American States Again. #MASA.

The winds of war have been blowing for some time. In fact, in *Federalist* 46, Madison warned of a "gathering storm" that would portend this battle between the two powers of federalism. This tempest would rain tyranny down on the heads of Americans were they to prove incapable of recognizing the darkening clouds of despotism. This storm would blow destructive and disastrous winds across the American political landscape, forever changing the face and the fate of the union of states.

The Federalist (known popularly as *The Federalist Papers*) — a collaboration of Madison, Alexander Hamilton and John Jay — were written to convince states to ratify the Constitution recently approved by state delegates at the convention in Philadelphia in 1787.

One of the obstacles impeding ratification was the objection of many noted and respected Americans. Patrick Henry, Madison's countryman and the silver-tongued Cicero of his day, was among the heroes of the struggle for independence from the British crown, and he was ferociously opposed to the adoption of the proposed Constitution. Henry and others — known to proponents as Anti-Federalists — felt obliged to warn the people of the latent threats to liberty they perceived in the product of Philadelphia.

On Monday, June 9, 1788, fewer than five months after *Federalist* 46 was published in New York, Patrick Henry rose for the third time at the convention and addressed the body of 168 delegates gathered in the Richmond Theatre in Richmond, Virginia to debate ratification of the newly proposed Constitution. In all, Henry delivered 24 discourses blasting away at the most "objectionable parts" of the Constitution.

In this particular speech, Henry summoned the specter of the "consolidating tendencies" which was haunting the proposed federal government. The great orator summoned his "poor abilities" to defend and ensure the sovereignty and survival of the state governments; Henry saw the future and forced his colleagues to look into the grim crystal ball he held:

> If consolidation proves to be as mischievous to this country as it has been to other countries, what will the poor inhabitants of this country do? This government will operate like an ambuscade. It will destroy the state governments, and swallow the liberties of the people, without giving previous notice.

These urgent and eloquent prophecies were similar in content and condemnation to the avalanche of arguments against the Constitution that James Madison had heard since the day the Constitution proposed by the Philadelphia convention was made public in September 1787.

In fact, when Madison sat down to draft *Federalist* 46 he likely believed that he had predicted and preempted all the threats to liberty his opponents claimed were lurking in the proposed constitution, threats like those Patrick Henry would bring up in June. It is interesting to note that James Madison would be in the room that hot day in June 1788 when Patrick Henry called out the Constitution and all its advocates for sneaking tyranny into the government by hiding it inside the Trojan Horse of a new constitution.

In *Federalist* 46, Madison addressed himself to those "adversaries of the Constitution" that an "uncontrolled" federal authority eventually would swallow up state governments and assume all state prerogatives.

Madison described a symbiotic relationship of state and federal government that would obviate a clash of powers. Madison believed that states would maintain their supremacy over the federal government in terms of their sovereignty principally through the effects of the greater attachment of the "affections" of the people to their state governments than to the distant federal authority.

History, it seems, has not borne out Madison's confidence in the connections of the people to their state governments.

Yet, Madison assumed that the people's devotion to their state legislatures would compel them to resist any effort by agents of the federal government to subordinate states to second-class status.

The people and the states, Madison argues, would never submit to such despotic designs. The power of this duo — inherent in the former and artificial in the latter — would prevent Patrick Henry's predicted consolidation of all political power by the federal government.

"What degree of madness," Madison asks incredulously, "could ever drive the federal government to such an extremity," to greedily encroach on the state governments?

There is an incredulous and dismissive tone to Madison's reassurances of the failsafe and organic potency of state governments. The people, he continued, would refuse to "cooperate with the officers of the union" who attempted to encroach on the prerogatives of the states; he genuinely believed that if the federal government were to take such a tyrannical tack, then states would combine to block the way, uniting to draw up "plans of resistance."

Besides, like those well-trained weather watchers that could detect the seed of a hurricane in a surging wave, Madison believed that the American people and the several states would see the "gathering storm" and prevent the precipitation of unchecked power and invasions on the rights of the people.

In this matter, Madison has proven less than oracular and we, his descendants, have proven to be useless as predictors of the currents and waves that are about to drown the states, the union, and liberty itself.

Why did James Madison (mis)place so much trust in his future countrymen? How did we descend to such (to Madison) an unfathomable and unhinged depth of societal delirium? How did we go from federal union of sovereign states to a consolidated "nation" ruled over by oligarchs? What steps led us to our current crisis? When did the states and the people decide to surrender sovereignty to an all-powerful plutocracy? And, more importantly, WHY did we watch while domestic enemies of freedom fiddled while our simple confederation burned and a complicated empire was built on the ashes?

Before beginning our study of the path toward tyranny Madison thought we'd never be crazy enough to trod, let's consider the following key to foretelling the future provided by the French author and philosopher, Charles Pinot Duclos:

> We see on the theater of the world a certain number of scenes which succeed each other in endless repetition: where we see the same faults followed regularly by the same misfortunes, we may reasonably think that if we could have known the first we might have avoided the others. The past should enlighten us on the future: knowledge of history is no more than an anticipated experience.

There was no better student of history among the Founders than James Madison and in *Federalist* 46 he recites a cursory review of European history, a history whose pages are stained with the blood of people once free who succumbed to the seductions of the power and prestige of empire. Then, after a few decades of decadence and the weakening of morals that it produces, the senses of the people were dulled and they made not a whimper as despots despoiled the people of their pride and their property.

In the last chapter of that continental chronicle, the people care for nothing other than the puerile and the pottage for which they cheaply sold their self-worth and their self-governing societies. With their collective memory erased by effeminacy, Europeans were left with but a little liberty and a lot less desire for that most celestial of objects.

After recounting this familiar tale of traitors turned tyrants and brave men turned timid subjects, Madison writes that he refuses to "insult the free and gallant citizens of America with the suspicion" that they would ever exchange their liberty for luxury.

Notice how Madison feels the need to soft-pedal his (to him ridiculous) predictions? James Madison was so sure that future Americans would never passively permit themselves to be carried along toward the abyss of absolutism; that they would never participate in the building — or fail to participate in the destruction — of an empire of ever-centripetal consolidation of power; that these people who disregarded pragmatic reasons to remain economic and moral slaves to monarchs and their multi-headed hydras of courtiers in order to cling to life in a wilderness; that these people whose ancestors tamed that wilderness and worked the land, causing it to bring forth bountiful harvests, would decay within decades into a slothful society who'd allow the general government to tax their income at the source and who'd pay billions to companies to pump filth into their homes; that these people would watch as an authoritarian government, funded by taxes taken from the people themselves, would build a Panopticon, placing every American under constant surveillance, in open rebellion of constitutional protections against such searches; etc., etc., etc.

This must be clear from the beginning of this short summary of the insanity Madison thought would never grip Americans: he genuinely believed what he wrote. Madison wasn't using hyperbole for political advantage. True, he was one of the primary promoters of the Constitution that created the government that Patrick Henry and others believed would "swallow up" all the liberties of the people, but no one would accuse Madison of being the master manipulator and inveterate liar that Alexander Hamilton, his Federalist co-author was known to be.

Readers should recognize right here at the beginning that I came neither to praise Madison nor to bury him. My sole and express purpose is to publicize the predictions Madison guarantees would never come true in America and, with great regret, to rehearse how the people of the united States (lower case "u" on purpose) have not only taken every single step toward tyranny that Madison mentions, but we have careered wildly, wantonly, and willfully down that psychotic street.

In order to convince delegates to the ratification conventions to ignore the frightening future painted by Patrick Henry and those of his opinion, Madison extracts from history five (as I reckon) completely unthinkable stages in the development of despotism that Americans would never allow to be copied from their continental cousins. After reading Madison's ridiculous record of how liberty is lost, Americans (specifically, the representatives at the ratification conventions considering the Constitution) would realize that there was no harm in joining the proposed "more perfect" union.

With the background of the battle in mind, let's get back to *Federalist* 46 and the "madness" Madison believed unimaginable.

Chapter 2

"Ambitious Encroachments:"
The Federal Government's Growth

A SSUMING YOU'RE sitting down, let's light this candle.

First, Madison argued that the people and the states would never elect men to the federal office "ready to betray" the best interest of both the states and the people.

Second, it was unthinkable to him that there would be "traitors" in the federal government who would vote to build up and maintain "a military establishment."

Third, Madison couldn't conceive that state legislatures would simply sit idly by as the federal government consolidated power, grabbing it almost unopposed from the states. Madison believed it was impossible that state governments would tolerate (much less support) a federal behemoth bent on making increasingly despotic demands of the states and the people.

Fourth, should the federal government somehow deceive the states and the people into aiding its accumulation of all power, the people, through the states, would recover their senses and "repel the danger" through a militia mustered and "fighting for their common liberties." These citizen-soldiers would form a popular armed force that Madison believed "could never be conquered."

And finally, state governments would form a living, legislative levee, a "barrier against the enterprises of ambition" undertaken by the federal government.

Madison could not be convinced that Americans would ever debase themselves to become "subjects of arbitrary power," too lazy to reclaim their hard-won liberty "from the hands of their oppressors." These heirs of the Revolution would never be brought to a state of "blind and tame submission to the long train of insidious measures" that would result in an all-powerful federal authority and the obliteration of the states as sovereign powers.

We, Madison's 21st Century posterity, are witnesses of the damage done by the perfect storm of the federal government's usurpation of unconstitutional power and the state governments' flaccid surrender of sovereignty. States willingly endure the federal flogging and then thank the federal rulers for the privilege of being beaten by their superiors. Then, they confirm their servitude by sending billions in tribute like sham regents of vassals of the all-powerful federal suzerain that *generously* tosses them scraps of sovereignty over a few residual areas of "strictly state concern." Ironically and tragically, the roles in the relationship between the states and federal government have been reversed and Washington considers the states expendable extras in its power play and state borders are drawn in chalk that dissolve and disappear under the steady, pounding rain of federal aggression.

Regarding Madison's list of events that would lead to this "great madness" and the abolition of state and popular sovereignty, one of the most applicable to our day and the most visible is the growth of the "military establishment." Madison assumed Americans would never allow "traitors" in the federal government to create this deadly industry.

According to data collected by the website MilitaryIndustrialComplex.com, from October 30, 2006 to November 2016, the federal government awarded over $2.8 TRILLION in defense contracts. In 2016 alone, the website claims, over $230 BILLION dollars have been paid to build up a military establishment that would strain the credulity of James Madison.

Of course, the recitation of the record-setting transfer of wealth from citizens to defense contractors is not the whole story. Consider the next arc in the cycle: money forcibly seized by the federal government from citizens is redirected to companies constructing the weapons of perpetual war. In turn, these companies donate millions to the campaign coffers of congressmen who then vote to award lucrative defense contracts to those companies. These companies then lean on their congressmen-cum-employees to whip up wars that create increased demand for these companies' war wares. It is an incestuous relationship that is as vile as it is vicious.

Next, despite Madison's confidence, not only is it not *rare* that we choose traitors to represent us, it is *common*. And it's not just unfaithful federal lawmakers and executives that are elected. Year after year we re-elect state lawmakers and governors who bow to the whims and wishes of Washington, hoping not to be left sucking hind tit when it comes time to suck money out of the fat federal sow.

These state legislators and governors bend over backward to avoid legal conflicts with federal statutes that, they believe, trump state laws. This unfounded belief is based on an incorrect reading of Article VI of the Constitution.

The Supremacy Clause (as some wrongly call it) of Article VI does not declare that federal laws are the supreme law of the land. It states that the Constitution "and laws of the United States made in pursuance thereof" are the supreme law of the land.

The phrase that pays is "In *pursuance* thereof, not "in *violation* thereof." If an act of Congress is not permissible under any enumerated power, it is not made in pursuance of the Constitution and therefore not only is *not* the supreme law of the land, it is not the law at all.

Alexander Hamilton put a fine point on the matter in *Federalist* 33:

But it will not follow from this doctrine that acts of the larger society which are *not pursuant* to its constitutional powers, but which are invasions of the residuary authorities of the smaller societies, will become the supreme law of the land. These will be merely acts of usurpation, and will deserve to be treated as such. [Emphasis in original.]

Acts not authorized under the enumerated powers of the Constitution are "merely acts of usurpations" and deserve to be disregarded, ignored, and denied any legal effect.

More state legislators need to learn this. Familiarity with these facts are fundamental to a reclaiming of state authority and removing the threat to liberty posed by the centralization of power in the federal government.

Until the states reassert the sovereignty they theoretically retain, there will be no end of the demands and they will get more and more difficult to comply with and will thus justify increasing federal control over the apparatuses of state government. The trajectory is easy to see and follow into the future. The federal government will mandate by mandate, regulation by regulation, grant program by grant program devolve into a central government after the model of the so-called European democracies.

The last item in Madison's list of things that states would never stand for is the disarming of state militias. As Madison saw it, should the unthinkable happen and the federal government overrun the high fences placed by the states around its enumerated powers, every foxhole in war over sovereignty would be filled with members of the state militias.

During the Virginia ratifying convention, James Madison described a standing army as the "greatest mischief that can happen." His colleague and fellow delegate to the Constitutional Convention of 1787, George Mason put a finer point on it:

No man has a greater regard for the military gentlemen than I have.

I admire their intrepidity, perseverance, and valor. But when once a standing army is established in any country, the people lose their liberty. When, against a regular and disciplined army, yeomanry are the only defence [sic], — yeomanry, unskilful and unarmed, — what chance is there for preserving freedom? Give me leave to recur to the page of history, to warn you of your present danger. Recollect the history of most nations of the world. What havoc, desolation, and destruction, have been perpetrated by standing armies!

In *Federalist*, No. 29, Alexander Hamilton echoes not only Mason's warning against a standing army, but his solution to the threat, as well:

If circumstances should at any time oblige the government to form an army of any magnitude that army can never be formidable to the liberties of the people while there is a large body of citizens, little, if at all, inferior to them in discipline and the use of arms, who stand ready to defend their own rights and those of their fellow-citizens. This appears to me the only substitute that can be devised for a standing army, and the best possible security against it, if it should exist.

In commenting on William Blackstone's *Commentaries on the Laws of England*, the founding era jurist and all-but-forgotten St. George Tucker speaks as if he foresaw our day and the fatal combination of an increasingly militarized police force and the disarmament of civilians:

"Wherever standing armies are kept up, and the right of the people to keep and bear arms is, under any colour or pretext whatsoever, prohibited, liberty, if not already annihilated, is on the brink of destruction."

The connection between this professional, civilian standing army and the attack on the right of the people to keep and bear arms has been recognized by contemporary liberty-minded scholars, as well.

In his essay, "The Right to Keep and Bear Arms Under the Second and Fourteenth Amendments: The Framers' Intent and Supreme Court Jurisprudence," Stephen Halbrook writes:

Noah Webster, the influential federalist whose name still appears on dictionaries, stated: "Before a standing army can rule, the people must be disarmed; as they are in almost every kingdom in Europe. The supreme power in America cannot enforce unjust laws by the sword; because the whole body of the people are armed... ." Pamphlets on the Constitution of the United States 56 (P. Ford ed. 1888).

In a similar treatise, Joyce Malcolm, a historian specializing in 17th century English constitutional history, makes the same point:

> Where does this leave the American Second Amendment, with its reference to a well-regulated militia necessary to the security of a free state, and its insistence that the right of the people to keep and bear arms shall not be infringed? I would argue that the Second Amendment mirrors English belief in the individual's right to be armed, the importance of that right to the preservation of liberty, and the preference for a militia over a standing army.

George Washington understood better than any of his contemporaries that a well-trained but otherwise ad hoc army composed of state militias could prove itself powerful enough to defeat the invading forces of a mighty empire. General Washington recognized the urgent need for a disciplined, organized, and independent state militia. As the continental commander-in-chief, Washington knew very well that training an army of citizen soldiers — many of whom used their muskets for little more than hunting — was crucial to restoring the freedom of America. In fact, it was the need for a more well-regulated force that compelled Washington to hire the Prussian officer, Friedrich von Steuben, to drill the soldiers of the Continental Army. His experience in the War for Independence likely inspired this statement, taken from his first annual address to Congress:

> A free people ought not only to be armed but disciplined; to which end a uniform and well digested plan is requisite: And their safety and interest require, that they should promote such manufactories, as tend to render them independent on others for essential, particularly for military supplies.

Most states have forgotten the historical role of state militias in the defense of freedom. They have failed to maintain an armed and disciplined militia capable of maintaining (or regaining) independence from tyrants.

Tim Baldwin, an attorney and author from Montana, commented ably on the failure of states to maintain a militia capable of repelling a federal armed force. Writes Baldwin:

> In spite of the Second Amendment's prescription that the States maintain a well-regulated militia to secure a "Free State" and the State constitutions and laws requiring State militias to protect the State's homeland, there is not one State that is capable of protecting the citizens from domestic or foreign invasion.

Baldwin is right. The mustering and maintenance of an organized militia, considered by Madison to be last line of defense against a tyrannical federal government, is often rejected even by many within the liberty movement.

The Founders (and all men who valued liberty) knew that the advantage of a citizen-militia over a professional standing army was that in militias, men fight for their families, their faith, and their freedom over their little plot of earth. The men of a militia are surrounded every day by that which is dearest and most divine to them, and they consider their defense of those things not to be an act of war, but an act of love. That is something that will never — can never — be understood by soldiers in a standing army deployed to foreign fields or fighting in wars where the mission seems missing in action.

Establishment types consider the subject to be an embarrassment and a fascination of the lunatic fringe of the right. Its advocates, they insist, should be shunned by all right-minded conservatives.

The plan to marginalize militias has been startlingly successful. There remain only 23 state defense forces (not including units of the National Guard and Reserve which are under the command of the president and are effectively just reserves of the federal armed forces). The problem, however, is that even these state-run militias are not militias in the sense that Madison and the founders were familiar with. They are nothing close to a citizen army that could be counted on to repel federal invasions.

In its decision in the 1990 case of *Perpich v. Department of Defense* 496 U.S. 334 (1990), the Supreme Court effectively federalized even state defense forces. The ruling, although explicitly claiming not to be ruling on the issue of the status of the state defense forces, referenced a few federal statutes that seem to support an inference of federalization of these ersatz militias.

The Supreme Court held:

It is true that the state defense forces 'may not be called, ordered, or drafted into the armed forces.' 32 U.S.C. 109(c). It is nonetheless possible that they are subject to call under 10 U.S.C. 331-333, which distinguish the 'militia' from the 'armed forces,' and which appear to subject all portions of the 'militia' - organized or not - to call if needed for the purposes specified in the Militia Clauses.

The following is a sample of the federal laws cited by the Supreme Court as being likely sources of federal government authority over state defense forces:

10 USC 331 - "Federal aid for State governments"

Whenever there is an insurrection in any State against its government, the President may, upon the request of its legislature or of its governor if the legislature cannot be convened, call into Federal service such of the militia of the other States, in the number requested by that State, and use such of the armed forces, as he considers necessary to suppress the insurrection.

10 USC 332 – "Use of militia and armed forces to enforce Federal authority"

Whenever the President considers that unlawful obstructions, combinations, or assemblages, or rebellion against the authority of the United States, make it impracticable to enforce the laws of the United States in any State or Territory by the ordinary course of judicial proceedings, he may call into Federal service such of the militia of any State, and use such of the armed forces, as he considers necessary to enforce those laws or to suppress the rebellion.

10 USC 333 – "Interference with State and Federal law"

The President, by using the militia or the armed forces, or both, or by any other means, shall take such measures as he considers necessary to suppress, in a State, any insurrection, domestic violence, unlawful combination, or conspiracy, if it –

(1) so hinders the execution of the laws of that State, and of the United States within the State, that any part or class of its people is deprived of a right, privilege, immunity, or protection named in the Constitution and secured by law, and the constituted authorities of that State are unable, fail, or refuse to protect that right, privilege, or immunity, or to give that protection; or

(2) opposes or obstructs the execution of the laws of the United States or impedes the course of justice under those laws.

In any situation covered by clause (1), the State shall be considered to have denied the equal protection of the laws secured by the Constitution.

As we all know, the Court is happy to give its sister branches an inch of authority through which they may take a mile of tyranny! That means that even the 23 state governments who have organized and mustered state defense forces in addition to the National Guard and Reserve units that are subordinate (in all meaningful ways) to the federal armed forces, have been gutted by the

Supreme Court. The *Perpich* decision (and others) reduced the independence of those forces, requiring them to accept the president as their commander or be deactivated.

Then, if any of these co-opted forces dare sound the call to defend their home states against the execution of unconstitutional federal mandates, they are subject to "suppression" by the president. I think we all know how liberally a president would interpret the scope and severity of that word.

Of course, today not only is the citizen-militia is a relic of a republican past, the right of a citizen to keep and bear arms as protected by the Second Amendment to the U.S. Constitution is now little more than a museum exhibition.

So, from the growth and gluttony of the military-industrial complex to the co-opting and disarming of independent state militias, all five elements of Madison's "long train of insidious measures" have arrived and the "great madness" afflicts nearly all state legislators and governors.

We have lost our way. We impotently rant about the tyranny of the federal government and its consolidation of power, yet we focus our efforts to restore liberty and the balance of power on the election of congressmen and presidents. We inexplicably look to Washington when we should be rebuilding our states and shoring up their sovereignty against the ferocious federal power grab that is only just beginning.

We know it won't happen, but very few of us are as concerned about the darkening rainclouds of despotism as Madison believed we would be.

States are not left defenseless in the battle to fight the cancer of consolidation. There is a remedy — a "rightful remedy" — that can immediately retrench the federal government's constant overreaching. This antidote can stop the poison of all unconstitutional federal acts and executive orders at the state borders and prevent them from working on the people.

The remedy for federal tyranny is nullification and applying it liberally will leave our states and our nation healthier and happier.

Chapter 3

Distinguishing the Creature from the Creator

UNDERSTANDING THAT the states created the federal government will help state legislators and citizens appreciate the constitutional propriety and potency of the principles of the Virginia and Kentucky Resolutions of 1798.

The states created the federal government and reserve the right to resist the exercise by Congress of any powers not specifically granted to it by the states in the Constitution. For too long, Congresses, presidents, judges, and bureaucrats have "worshipped and served the creature [the government] more than the creator [the states and the people]." (Romans 1:25)

This wasn't always the case. Three decades after Madison and Jefferson wrote the Kentucky and Virginia Resolutions, U.S. Senator John Rowan of Kentucky delivered what in the opinion of many is the most insightful and persuasive speech among those collectively considered as part of the Webster-Hayne debates.

After listening to Daniel Webster of Massachusetts and his New England allies fabricate a false history of the formation of the union of American states, Rowan explained that the states created the Constitution and that the people are represented in the federal government in their collective capacity as states.

Before sharing Senator Rowan's remarks, it's important to expose that the claims made by Daniel Webster (the man declared the winner of the debate by every history textbook) about the way the states came together under the Constitution were not only completely untrue, but that it is likely Webster knew it.

First, the statements made by Daniel Webster that I'm about to quote were not made during the Webster-Hayne debates that took place in 1830. Webster made these statements a few years later (February 16, 1833, for those who want to look them up) in a response to a discourse delivered by Senator John Calhoun of South Carolina.

To be honest, though, that doesn't matter. The point of publishing Webster's version of the creation of the union was accepted as the truth by many northern lawmakers in the decades leading up to the War for Southern Independence (1861-1865) and by most Americans in the decades since that war ended.

Now, I present Daniel Webster's own words, followed by the irrefutable record of the ratification debates that will prove he prevaricated, maybe knowingly.

Referring to remarks made by John Calhoun, Daniel Webster said:

The sense of the gentleman's proposition, therefore, is not at all affected, one way or the other, by the use of this word. That proposition still is, that out system of government is but a *compact* between the people of separate and sovereign States.

Was it Mirabeau, Mr. President, or what other master of the human passions, who has told us that words are things? They are indeed things, and things of mighty influence, not only in addresses to the passions and high wrought feelings of mankind, but in the discussion of legal and political questions also; because a just conclusion is often avoided, or a false one reached, by the adroit substitution of one phrase, or one word, for another. Of this we have, I think, another example in the resolutions before us.

The first resolution declares that the people of the several States "*acceded*" to the Constitution, or to the constitutional compact, as it is called. This word "*accede*," not found either in the Constitution itself, or in the ratification of it by any one of the States, has been chosen for use here, doubtless not without a well-considered purpose.

The natural converse of *accession* is *secession*; and, therefore, when it is stated that the people of the States *acceded* to the Union, it may be more plausibly argued that they may *secede* from it. If, in adopting the constitution, nothing was done but acceding to a *compact*, nothing would seem necessary, in order to break it up, but to secede from the same compact. (All emphases in original)

So, just in case you missed it, in his speech refuting one made by John Calhoun, Daniel Webster claimed that the words "accede" and "accession" were never used during the debates on the ratification of the Constitution. Never. used.

Here's the truth:

On Wednesday, February 6, 1788, Samuel Stillman said:

From all that has been said on the subject of biennial elections, it is my decided opinion that two years in the general government will not be in proportion to one year in the local governments; because, in the former, the objects of government will be great, numerous, and extensive; in the latter, comparatively small and limited. The general government involves all the states now in the Union — all such as shall in future **accede** to it….(Emphasis added)

Reverend Samuel Stillman delivered this speech during the debates on ratification of the Constitution held in **BOSTON, MASSACHUSETTS!**

You know, Massachusetts, the state Daniel Webster represented in the Senate, the Senate where he claimed — after making a big deal about how people pretend words were used just to serve their selfish interests — that the word "accede" was never spoken once at any of the ratification debates!

One more example of the use of the word "accede" will suffice for the purpose of this chapter.

On Wednesday, June 25, 1788, delegate John Lansing made the following statement during a speech at the ratification convention of the state of New York:

> I presume I shall not be charged with rashness, I continue to insist that it is still our duty to maintain our rights. We acknowledge that our dissent cannot prevent the operation of the government: since nine states have **acceded** to it, let them make the experiment. (Emphasis added)

So, in summary, Daniel Webster said the Constitution and the general government it defines was never acceded to by the states. He said that the words "accede" or "accession" were never heard at any of the state ratification debates. Then, Webster explained why he so adamantly (and arrogantly) claimed that those words were never used: "If, in adopting the constitution, nothing was done but acceding to a *compact*, nothing would seem necessary, in order to break it up, but to secede from the same compact." (Emphasis in original)

Well said, Mr. Webster, well said.

Now, back to the eloquent — and completely truthful — speech delivered on February 4, 1830 from the floor of the U.S. Senate by John Rowan of Kentucky. It's a little long, but, in light of the lack of understanding by 21st Century Americans of the true history of this confederated republic, it is worth reading every word:

> I rose mainly to enter my solemn protest against some of the political doctrines advanced by the honorable gentleman from Massachusetts (Mr. Webster.) He has asserted, in the course of this debate, that the constitution of the United States was not formed by the States; that it is not a compact formed by the States, but a government formed by the people; that it is a popular government, formed by the people at large; and he adds, "that if the whole truth must be told, they brought it into existence, established it, and have hitherto supported it, for the very purpose, among others, of imposing certain salutary restraints on State

sovereignties."

He asserts further, that in forming the General Government, the people conferred upon the Supreme Court of the United States, the power of imposing these certain salutary restraints upon the sovereignty of the States. Now, Sir, believing as I do, most solemnly, that these doctrines strike at the root of all our free institutions, and lead directly to a consolidation of the Government, I cannot refrain from attempting, however feeble the attempt may be, to expose their fallacy, and their dangerous tendency. It is the first time they have been openly avowed, (so far as I have been informed,) in either House of Congress. They were thought to be fairly inferrible [sic], from the tenor and import of the first message of the late President Adams, to the Congress; but they were left to inference, [267] and were not explicitly avowed. The recommendation of Secretary Rush, that the industry of the people should be regulated by Congress, must have been predicated upon his belief, and that of Mr. Adams, in these doctrines. But still the friends of Mr. Adams, when these doctrines were imputed to him, and his message quoted in support of the imputation, resisted it with warmth, and ascribed the inferences from the message, and from the report of Secretary Rush, to unkind or party feelings. Now, the explicit avowal of the honorable Senator, (Mr. W.) removes all doubt from the subject. We can no longer doubt as to what was the political faith of Mr. Adams. His most zealous and most distinguished apostle has avowed it. The two parties are now clearly distinguishable, by their opposite political tenets; the one headed by our illustrious Chief Magistrate, who is the friend and advocate of the rights of the States; the other party is now headed by the honorable Senator from Massachusetts, (Mr. Webster,) and is, as I shall contend, and attempt to prove, in favor of a consolidation of the Government—of a splendid Empire. The doctrine avowed is neither more nor less than that the State sovereignties are merely nominal, and that the Government was consolidated in its formation. How it has happened, that this essential characteristic of the Government was so long kept a secret from the people of the States, is a matter of some mystery. Why was it not avowed at the time the Constitution was formed? Why was this disclosure reserved until this time, and for this occasion? Is there any thing in the message of the President, or in the political condition of the people of the States, which demands its promulgation at this time? Are the people prepared, think you, to receive an entire new version of their Constitution? Will they give up their dependence upon their States respectively, and rely upon the great Central Government for the protection of their lives, liberty, and property? Sir, I think not; they are not yet sufficiently tamed and subdued, by the aristocracy of the land, and the encroachments of the General Government upon the rights of the States, to submit just at once.

Mr. President, I would ask the honorable Senator how his doctrine can be correct, consistently with the known state of facts, at the time the Constitution was formed. What was the condition of the people at that time? Were they at large, and unconnected by any political ties whatever? Or were they in a state of self government under distinct political associations? It is known to every body, that the people consisted of, and constituted thirteen distinct, independent, and sovereign States. That those States were connected together by a compact of Union, and that the great object of the [268] people of the States, informing the Constitution, was that declared in its preamble, to make the Union more perfect. What union, I would ask, or union of what? Most certainly of the States, already united, whose union was thought to be imperfect. To give more compaction, and render more perfect, the Union of the States, was the great desideratum. To consolidate the union of the States was the object of the constitutional compact.

Nearly three years later, none of that would be remembered.

On November 24, 1832, state legislators in John Calhoun's home state of South Carolina declared that the federal tariffs of 1828 and 1832 were "unauthorized by the Constitution of the United States and violate the true meaning and intent thereof" and that the State of South Carolina considered such unconstitutional acts to be "null and void, and no law...."

On December 10, some 17 days later, President Andrew Jackson issued a proclamation that South Carolina's resolution was "incompatible with the existence of the Union, contradicted expressly by the letter of the Constitution...."

In 1832, Edward Livingston of New York was serving as the Secretary of State in the Jackson administration. Livingston is believed by many to be the co-author of Jackson's Proclamation.

While serving in the U.S. Senate, though, Livingston delivered a discourse very discordant with the "facts" recited by Andrew Jackson in the Proclamation of 1832.

On February 29, 1830 — during the aforementioned Webster-Hayne debates — Senator Livingston wrote that the state pre-existed the Constitution and thus pre-existed the federal government. He explained that the federal government was not created until the Constitution was ratified by the states.

The states existed before the Constitution; they parted only with such powers as are specified in that instrument; they continue still to exist with all the powers they have not ceded, and the present Government, would never, itself, gone into operation, had not the States, in their political capacity, have consented.

As an extension of this pedigree of power, Livingston declared that were a state to be injured by some usurpation of power by the federal government, then that state "would have a right at once to declare that it would no longer be bound by a compact which had been grossly violated."

Just over a year separated this declaration by Livingston and the proclamation of President Andrew Jackson.

Were Livingston sitting in the Senate today, he would witness every day many of his colleagues "grossly violat[ing]" the Constitution. He would watch one after the other congresses repeatedly and unrepentantly exercising powers not granted them by the states in the compact called the Constitution.

Jefferson, Madison, Livingston, and others would encourage states to demand that the government of the United States cease the constant abuse of power and conform itself to confine their activities within those boundaries drawn by state representatives in the Constitution and later agreed to by separate ratifying conventions in the states.

Regarding the ratification of the proposed constitution by the states, the documents sent by the states to Congress announcing their ratification (or rejection) of the Constitution provide additional evidence of the founding generation's appreciation of the states' and federal government's respective roles as creator and creation. In nearly every one of these letters, the state legislature or ratifying convention delegation explicitly remind Congress that the consent of the states formed the federal government.

Delaware, for example, declared:

We the Deputies of the People of the Delaware State, in Convention met, having taken into our serious consideration the Federal Constitution proposed and agreed upon by the Deputies of the United States in a General Convention held at the City of Philadelphia....

New Jersey expressed a similar understanding of the parties to the constitutional compact:

Whereas a convention of Delegates from the following States, vizt. New Hampshire, Massachusetts, Connecticut, New York, New Jersey, Pennsylvania, Delaware, Maryland, Virginia, North Carolina, South Carolina and Georgia, met at Philadelphia for the purpose of deliberating on, and forming a constitution for the United States of America....

Georgia's ratification notice letter also recorded the states' role as creators of the new federal government:

> Whereas the form of a Constitution for the Government of the United States of America, was, on the seventeenth day of September, one thousand seven hundred and eighty-seven, agreed upon and reported to Congress by the Deputies of the said United States convened in Philadelphia....

New York's notice of ratification explicitly expressed that state's power to reassume the full panoply of its political powers should the government created in the Constitution fail to maintain the happiness of her people:

> That the Powers of Government may be reassumed by the People, whensoever it shall become necessary to their Happiness....

Going further, New York's ratification letter laid out the precise limits of federal authority:

> [E]very Power, Jurisdiction and right, which is not by the said Constitution clearly delegated to the Congress of the United States, or the departments of the Government thereof, remains to the People of the several States, or to their respective State Governments to whom they may have granted the same....

On February 6, 1788 Massachusetts agreed to assent to the proposed constitution provided that a roster of recommended amendments be made to the document the state's ratification convention was being asked to accept.

The first of the nine amendments suggested by the state's ratification convention delegates would add the following limit to the Constitution (a restriction that would — more or less — be included in the Tenth Amendment that would be added to the Constitution in 1789):

> That it be explicitly declared that all Powers not expressly delegated by the aforesaid Constitution are reserved to the several States to be by them exercised.

New Hampshire's ratification notice contained the same suggested amendment in almost identical language.

Finally, Virginia — the oldest of the British colonies among the thirteen — made it very clear where power came from and where it would return to should the federal government ever exceed the limits of its authority as set forth in the Constitution. The letter from the Old Dominion to Congress declares:

We the delegates of the people of Virginia...in behalf of the People of Virginia declare and make known that the powers granted under the Constitution being derived from the People of the United States may be resumed by them whensoever the same shall be perverted to their injury or oppression and that every power not granted thereby remains with them and at their will: that therefore no right of any denomination can be cancelled abridged restrained or modified by the Congress by the Senate or House of Representatives acting in any Capacity by the President or any Department or Officer of the United States except in those instances in which power is given by the Constitution for those purposes....

And on, and on, and on. The ratifying conventions called throughout the thirteen states understood that the delegates sent to Philadelphia in the summer of 1787 created a general government of limited power, retaining for themselves undiminished right to resume all political power they exercised successfully for over a century.

If nullification is to be successfully deployed and defended, states' lawmakers must remember that the Constitution is a creature of the states and that the federal government was given very few and very limited powers over objects of national importance. Any act of Congress, the courts, or the president that exceeds that small scope is null, void, and of no legal effect. No exceptions.

James Madison said it best in *Federalist* 45, "The powers delegated by the proposed Constitution to the federal government, are few and defined. Those which are to remain in the State governments are numerous and indefinite."

These federal deprivations of fundamental rights is nothing less that patricide by a thousand paper cuts. That is what the constant wounds inflicted by the federal government on the Constitution amount to. The child watches the parent, witnesses its lethargy and ascribes it to the parent having grown weak and flabby, unable to fight back. Sensing the hour of its ascension has come, the child delivers body blow after body blow, forcing the father to his knees. Then, the final kick to the face and the father comes to his own realization: he can't control his offspring.

Have we come to this? How long will the states and the people absorb the punches of the federal government? Have we become so accustomed to the abuse that we've forgotten how to defend ourselves? Will we now just cede our natural right to rule and allow the creature to command the creator?

Chapter 4

Constitution as a Compact

THE STATES CREATED the federal government, set the boundaries of its power, and reserved to themselves all other rights not specifically delegated to the new national authority. The contract containing the rights and responsibilities of the parties to this contract that created the federal government is called the Constitution . This act of collective consenting is called a compact.

This element of the creation of the union is precisely where the states derive their power to negative acts of the federal government that exceed its constitutional authority. It is a thread woven inextricably in every strand of sovereignty. It was the sovereign states that ceded the territory of authority which the federal government occupies.

Despite the heft of the historical evidence supporting the compact theory of constitutional construction, there are those who deny that the Constitution is a compact between sovereign and independent states. James Wilson, a lawyer, distinguished founder, and delegate to the convention in Philadelphia pointed to the phrase "We, the People" in the preamble as proof that the Constitution was the creation of the people, not the states. Given Wilson's prominence and participation in the constitutional convention, deference is often given to his opinions.

James Madison is no lesser authority than Wilson when it comes to the constitutional convention, however, and the notes he wrote of the proceedings of that event paint a different picture of the process that culminated in the Constitution and the formation of the federal government.

For example, in the original version of the preamble, a roster of the names of the several states were listed, identifying them as the parties that intended to "ordain and establish" the Constitution.

The final version of the preamble, however, declares that "We, the People" not we, the states, ordained and established the Constitution. Regardless of the nationalists' fascination with this paragraph, they have once again hitched their wagon to the wrong horse.

To prove it, study how the preamble was drafted. As originally agreed upon by the convention delegates, the preamble read:

We the people of the states of New Hampshire, Massachusetts, Rhode Island and Providence Plantations, Connecticut, New York, New Jersey, Pennsylvania, Delaware, Maryland, Virginia, North Carolina, South Carolina, and Georgia, do ordain, declare, and establish the following Constitution for the government of ourselves and our posterity.

Nowhere in Madison's record of the proceedings of the convention (or that of the others who made similar sketches) is the process that led to the alteration from "we the people of the states" to "we the people" explained. We do know that Gouvernor Morris was the head of the committee of detail that ultimately put the final polish on the Constitution. Morris was a man renowned for his political savvy (as well as his way with the ladies). The delegates trusted his deftness with a pen and submitted the rough draft to him to be cleaned up.

We also know that above all things, James Madison and Alexander Hamilton wanted the Constitution to be ratified by the states, so they probably didn't fret much over the change. As Madison was the unofficial chronicler of the convention, it is no wonder, therefore, that we have no record of any argument over the lopping off of the "of the states" in the opening phrase of the preamble.

Political pragmatists that they were, Madison and Hamilton understood that ratification by all the states named in the first draft of the preamble was unlikely. In fact, ratification in Virginia and New York — the home states of Madison and Hamilton respectively — was not a foregone conclusion and would both these large states would be what would we call "battleground states" in the ratification process.

So, rather than enumerate states to a union that some of them might never join, Morris finessed the phraseology to include the states collectively without naming them individually.

In light of this realpolitik consideration, it is little wonder that the phrases of the preamble were tweaked in order to grease the skids leading to the formation of a more perfect union.

This timely edit did not reflect, however, a deeper shift in the founders' understanding of the roles of states in the process of empowering a federal authority. As constitutional scholar Williams J. Watkins, Jr. has noted, "The debates in no way indicate a change in theory took place ...."

In fact, the Constitution's prescribed method of its own ratification reveals that a plurality of states, not citizens, would be required before the document became the law of the land.

Not once during the deliberations at the Constitutional Convention was there a proposal that their work be presented for approval to the body of the populace acting as individuals. From the beginning of the process that culminated on September 17, 1787 with the signing of the Constitution, it was understood that the ratification by at least nine states was the *sine qua non* of the start of the new government.

Still, the ranks of the Establishment are full of compact theory deniers who obstinately deny one irrefutable fact: The Constitution never would have gone into legal effect and the federal government never would have been created if state conventions had not met and ratified the document.

In fact, the first congress would never have considered a single bill if their authority was recognized by a supermajority of Americans, but rejected by the state ratifying conventions. Not even the most zealous supporters of the Constitution would have assumed that the new government would have been authorized to act — would have been in any way legally binding — by an affirmative vote by the people of the states.

There are two reasons why a popular vote would never had been accepted as a substitute for state ratification. First, the Constitution itself contains no mechanism for popular ratification. Second, the people, since the earliest days of their resistance to British tyranny, had expressed their opposition through their collective capacity as colonies or states.

Review the record of the rebellion: Albany Plan of Union, Declaration of Independence, Continental Congress, Articles of Confederation, etc. None of these milestones on the road to independence were written, voted on, ratified, or sent to King George by "the American people." They were sent in the name of the organized political units the American had already formed — the states.

Another equally important question is why Americans always acted as states and colonies rather than as a people, taking votes, counting the yeas and nays, and appending their names to petitions. The answer lies in the definition and locus of sovereignty.

Sovereignty is the "supreme and independent power or authority in government as possessed or claimed by a state or community." Americans of the founding generation, and for a century before that, firmly held that sovereignty rested in the representative bodies they formed. Did the Mayflower pilgrims, for example, land in American and begin dealing individually with Mother England? Did the Jamestown have a colonists on their own or in their own names communicate with the crown and Parliament? No. Houses of Burgesses, committees, etc. were the vehicles chosen by American Britons to convey their concerns to London.

It is important to insert at this point a proposition put to me by many in the liberty community regarding popular sovereignty. There is a small, but animated segment of the libertarian political spectrum that argues that citizens need not rely on states to nullify unconstitutional federal acts, but individuals can do so on their own. That is to say, a person would not have to hope his state legislature and governor would approve legislation denying participation in Obamacare, for example, rather he could simply refuse to do so on his own, an act this group claims is their right as natural sovereigns.

There is one historical and constitutional problem with this position. Never, neither in the history of the settlement of the American colonies, nor in their history of regaining their independence and subsequent union as states is there an example of citizens resisting tyranny in their capacity as individuals. As explained above, every time these former Englishmen pushed back against the crown's consolidation of power, it was done in the name of the colonies, not the colonists.

Nullification (and secession), therefore, rests safely on a sound constitutional foundation when it is exercised by people in their collective political expression as states.

That said, it is true that the people possess ultimate sovereignty. As the natural rulers, the people delegated certain powers of governance to their state legislatures. These state governments, in turn, sublet some portion of that power to a general government they created to handle external affairs. James Madison economically explained this unique power sharing arrangement in *Federalist* 46, "The federal and state governments are in fact but different agents and trustees of the people...."

In light of the foregoing history of America's establishment of government, official opposition to English oppression, the accepted definition and location of sovereignty, and the method of ratification set forth in Article VII of the Constitution the strength of the argument against the states' retention of all but a few specifically listed powers is enervated.

Once we realize that state governments are the collective expression of popular sovereignty and that the Constitution is a compact entered into by these duly empowered representatives of the people, the inquiry moves on to the scope of the new central government's power as contained within the four corners of that agreement. A sound understanding of those enumerated powers is key to knowing when and why states are justified in ignoring (or, if they decide to, nullify) acts of the federal government.

Nullification, whether through active acts passed by the legislatures or the simple refusal to obey unconstitutional directives, is the "rightful remedy" for the ill of federal usurpation of authority. Americans committed to the Constitution must walk the fences separating the federal and state governments and they must keep the former from crossing into the territory of the latter.

The Virginia and Kentucky Resolutions plainly set forth James Madison's and Thomas Jefferson's understanding of the source of all federal power. Those landmark documents clearly demonstrate what these two agile minded champions of liberty considered the constitutional delegation of power. Jefferson summed it up very economically in the Kentucky Resolutions:

> That the several states who formed that instrument, being sovereign and independent, have the unquestionable right to judge of its infraction; and that a nullification, by those sovereignties, of all unauthorized acts done under colour [sic] of that instrument, is the rightful remedy ....

Madison and Jefferson recognized that honest men could and would disagree about the proper interpretation of this or that constitutional provision. Not all of these men would be trying purposefully to enlarge the size and scope of the central government, some would merely be applying their own set of principles to resolving issues of constitutional construction. In these cases, Madison and Jefferson recommended the Principles of '98 as an accurate lens through which adversaries should view the Constitution.

No serious debate should be entertained as to whether the national authority has repeatedly attempted to break down the boundaries placed by the Constitution around its power. From the beginning, our elected representatives have overstepped the limits drawn around their rightful authority and have passed laws retracting, reversing, and redefining the scope of American liberty and state sovereignty. Our sacred duty is to tirelessly resist such advances and exercise all our natural rights to restrain government and keep it within the limits set by the Constitution.

In his speech on the bank bill delivered in 1791, Madison said, "In controverted cases, the meaning of the parties to the instrument, if collected by reasonable evidence, is a proper guide."

Thomas Jefferson similarly argued that the Constitution should be interpreted "according to the true sense in which it was adopted by the states, that in which it was advocated by its friends, and not that which its enemies apprehended."

If one were to assume that the Constitution is not an agreement among equals, then one must also accept the corollary that the states are mere subordinates of the federal government without the right to seek a remedy to the wrongs perpetrated by the plutocrats on the Potomac. The states, as dissatisfied children, would have to submit to their parent government, with no more morally acceptable remedy than to complain and to bristle.

However, sovereignty is not an either/or proposition. The states are the possessors of original governing sovereignty (as an aggregation of the popular political will) and they created another government with powers derived from their own. The government of the United States was not created *ex nihilo*.

Understanding the facts of its formation demonstrate that although the government of the United States is a separate entity, it is not, indeed cannot be, superior to the states. Such a suggestion is illogical and there is not a single sentence of support for this supposition in all the annals of the history of the creation of the federal government.

This concept is succinctly set forth by Alexander Stephens in his book, *A Constitutional View of the Late War Between the States*. In this landmark two-volume treatise examining the causes and effects of the Civil War through a constitutional lens, Stephens explains, "Only sovereign states could endow a common government with sovereignty."

It's that simple. State governments could not create a general authority with any degree of power unless they held that power in at least an equal degree prior to the latter's creation. Put another way, could the states give the federal government something they themselves did not already possess? The very thought is ludicrous!

To better appreciate this concept, take it down to the personal level. It is logical and apparent to anyone that I can't give one of my neighbors permission to rummage through the garage of another neighbor, because I don't have that power myself. I can't give my neighbor permission to paint another neighbor's house because I don't have that right, either.

I could, however, give my neighbor permission to paint my own house because I have unquestionable authority over my own property.

Why do we fail to breakdown these questions of sovereignty and power into more manageable questions that every man, woman, and child could understand and give correct and rational answers?

The answer is that those whose petty empires crumble under the weight of that logic are in a position to prevent such simple explanations from ever reaching the ears of those who would otherwise join the army of liberty. These oligarchs control the curricula taught in public schools, they control the news broadcast by the media, and they control the stories printed by the press. Were it not for independent media and the internet, the ramparts of these castles of consolidation would be unassailable.

In addition to the record of the drafting of the Constitution, the compact theory of the formation of the union is also supported by the history of the events that led to the calling of the convention of 1787.

After successfully passing through the trial of the War for Independence, having affirmed thereby their inalienable right of self-government, the 13 former colonies exercised their sovereignty by making compacts with other states.

The first of these agreements was a "firm league of friendship" known as the Articles of Confederation. The members of this new confederacy established a body endowed with power to legislate in a few areas of mutual interest while retaining the lion's share of sovereign powers.

The states explicitly explained in the contracting instrument that no independently sovereign, sui generis, national government was contemplated or created.

The purpose for the formation of the confederacy was to unite themselves for their mutual benefit in a "perpetual union," not to surrender their hard won sovereignty through the midwifing of an embryonic despot, born with the potential to grow into an annihilator of rights similar to the fully fledged one they had so recently banished from their shores. To believe there was such an intent would require a suspension of reason and ignorance of the causes and goals of the War for Independence.

Admittedly, the centrifugal forces flinging the states away from the confederacy were more powerful than many anticipated and the ties that lashed the states together were rapidly loosening. The factors hastening this dissolution are well known.

Primarily, the states were concerned with how to enforce an equitable distribution of the obligation to repay the debts incurred to finance the war with Britain. In the vacuum of a suitable settlement, chaos grew, as well as an American credibility deficit overseas.

This weakened position convinced a majority of the founding generation that their newly restored republics were vulnerable to foreign aggression, especially from England.

To avoid having to fight for freedom every year, the hero of the war and "father of his country," George Washington, hosted a conference at his home, Mt. Vernon. The goal of the gathering was to resolve border and trading disputes between Virginia and Maryland. While resulting in no substantial agreement between representatives of the neighboring states, there was a sense that a larger convention — one where more states would be invited — might have enough clout to solve the pressing issues of common concern, principally that of self-preservation.

The first significant attempt at holding such a meeting was the conference that came to be known as the Annapolis Convention. At Annapolis, Maryland in September 1786, 12 delegates from five states (Delaware, New Jersey, Pennsylvania, Virginia, and New York) came together for the express purpose of hammering out some workable solution to the problems of international trade, interstate relations, and the weaknesses of the Articles of Confederation. Looking through the lens of history we see that the most important product of this mini-convention was the drafting by Alexander Hamilton of a report. In this document, the future Philadelphia delegate and co-author of the *Federalist* proposed to the Confederation Congress that a larger, more official meeting be convened in

Philadelphia in May 1787 for the purpose of "considering the situation of the United States" including a mandate "to devise such further provisions as shall appear to them necessary to render the constitution of the federal government adequate to the exigencies of the union...."

Remarkably, even to a master manipulator like Hamilton, Congress heeded the call and proposed that states send delegates to Philadelphia "for the purpose of revising the Articles of Confederation."

It is in the details of these calls for convention that we find language relevant to the nature of the American union and who were the parties to its formation.

The call from Congress was sent not to the people, but to the state governments. The state legislatures were invited to send a delegation to help repair rips in the constitutional fabric. This historical fact is irrefutable evidence that a functioning agreement for a government of the United State was the goal. That government, if it was to exist at all, would be the creation of the states that participated in the formation of it.

Additional evidence of the claim that the states were the only interested parties in the compact of the Constitution is found in the way votes were taken and recorded at the convention in Philadelphia. Representatives voted as states, not as individuals. In fact, the journal where those votes were recorded catalogs the yeas and nays according to the name of state, not the name of the delegate.

Another clue to the identity of the parties to the Constitution, is found in Articles V and VII of the document itself.

Article V requires that amendments be "ratified by the legislatures of three-fourths of the states or by conventions in three-fourths thereof." Not only was the Constitution a binding contract among the states, but any alterations of the provisions of that contract had to be signed off by a supermajority of the parties.

Next, the prose and purpose of Article VII makes the issue so clear as to permit no reasonable alternative interpretation. In this brief statement the role of the states as the sine qua non of the Constitution is established. Article VII reads, "The Ratification of the Conventions of nine States, shall be sufficient for the Establishment of this Constitution between the States so ratifying the Same."

Plainly and purposefully the framers of the Constitution recognized that the document they signed in September 1787 was an agreement among the states represented. Every article was written by the states, voted on by the states, accepted or rejected by the states, ultimately approved by the states, and it would only become binding upon states who ratified it.

Why were the people not polled or asked to vote up or down on the Constitution? Because this was neither a popular nor a national compact; it was a compact creating a confederation of sovereign states.

As constitutional attorney Kent Masterson Brown explains, "The idea that the constitution that they [the framers] had drafted and ratified was entered into 'by the people,' as opposed to the states, and was irrevocable once ratified was absolutely unknown to the framers and ratifiers."

I would add that had these men been convinced that such an arrangement was advocated or even so much as contemplated by those pushing for acceptance of the Constitution, it never would have been ratified by the requisite number of states and the embryonic American confederation would have been still born in Philadelphia.

Had the Constitution somehow survived, a cursory review of the history of the time between the close of the Philadelphia convention and the ratification by the states of the Constitution reveals that had the people had the determining vote as to whether the Constitution should have been adopted, it never would have happened.

The foregoing survey of the historical record of the calling of the Constitutional Convention of 1787, the method prescribed for its establishment as the union's founding charter, and the plain text of Articles V and VII reveals that those who wrote it and signed off on it understood the Constitution to be a compact among the sovereign states that ratified it. As parties to the contract, the states are safely within their legal right, therefore, to demand that the agreed upon terms be strictly enforced and that the federal government was kept within the fences erected in that agreement.

Those of us enlisted in this fight will see our ranks grow as we take the time to share the *true* story of how the union was brought into being. When those predisposed to defend liberty understand the nature of the relationship of the states to the federal and how the latter only exists as a result of a compact created and agreed to by the former, they will grow stronger and braver to stand up for themselves. They will no longer collapse under the barrage of jabs thrown by the federal government and they will resume their rightful role as creator.

Chapter 5

Applying Contract Law to Compact Theory

IN ORDER TO HELP friends of liberty tightly grasp the compact theory that informs the Constitution, I'll make a couple of legal analogies that will be more familiar to 21st Century Americans.

First, it is a well settled principle of Anglo-American law that parties to a contract may rightfully seek remedies if another party is in breach of the agreed upon terms. One such remedy available to an aggrieved party is to require that the party in breach amend his behavior to conform to the terms of the contract. The aggrieved party may point to the violated provisions of the contract and remind the offending party of the obligations undertaken in the contract.

This reasonable approach is analogous to nullification. As the aggrieved parties, the states (or a single state) may remind the federal government of its repeated violations of key terms of the original agreement and demand that it cease such excesses and that it restrain itself according to the mutually approved contractual rights and responsibilities.

Despite the reasonableness of this recourse, states have been reluctant to take this intermediate step toward forcing the feds back within their proper boundaries of power.

At this point it is important to point out that the Constitution is **not** a contract between the states as one party and the federal government as another, with the rights and responsibilities of each party spelled out in the provisions of the agreement.

That's not the way it happened at all. The Constitution is a contract among the states wherein they agreed to create a separate, subordinate entity to serve their common interests. This distinction is critical to interpreting the language of and understanding the purpose of the Constitution and the articles and clauses it contains.

The legal arrangement created by this contract (the Constitution) is that of principal and agent and will be discussed a little later in this chapter.

Returning to the analysis of the remedies available to the states as parties to a contract, there is, of course, another more aggressive contractual remedy available in the corpus of contract law. If one party to the contract suffers consistent breaches of a contract, he may seek rescission of the entire agreement.

Rescission is defined as the cancellation of a contract and is customarily followed by restitution. Restitution is the return of the parties to their pre-contractual position, the position they were in prior to entering into the contract relationship.

Whereas the first remedy is analogous to nullification, rescission is comparable to secession. States, as aggrieved parties, are safely within their long-established rights in common law to abandon the union and reassume the full panoply of powers and privileges it earlier ceded to the general government in the contract (the Constitution). The newly-separated states would be once again free to remain independent republics or to enter into another contractual relationship (confederacy) with one or more states similarly separated from the union they once formed a part of.

While this path is open to the states, it isn't always necessary. Truthfully, no one who has witnessed the repeated violations of the terms of the original compact by the federal government would blame the states for severing the ties that bind them to that inveterate tyrant.

That said, there are yet millions of Americans who recognize the genius of the Constitution and earnestly want it to succeed, not only just for the sake of political stability, but for the sake of demonstrating deference to the founding generation who took the time to distill the wisdom of ages into that unique document.

To sum up, should a state or states decide not to continue silently suffering constant breaches of that agreement by one of the other parties or by the any one of the parts of the general government created by it, they may lawfully demand a halt to the offending behavior and a performance by the breaching party of its contractual obligations.

If the breaches are significant enough, however, the states may demand rescission of the entire contract and return to their pre-contractual position. And remember, there is no requirement that the states expressly retain this right of rescission in the agreement — it is available as an independent operation of law. Madison was no lawyer, but he knew and understood this legal principle. In fact, he summed it up perfectly in a speech he made at the Philadelphia convention:

> Clearly, according to the expositors of the law of nations, that a breach of any one article, by any one party, leaves all other parties at liberty to consider the whole convention to be dissolved, unless they choose rather to compel the delinquent party to repair the breach.

In the first volume of his *Commentaries on the Laws of England* published in 1753, the inimitable jurist Sir William Blackstone clearly defined the proper relationship and chronology of creation of the rights possessed naturally by human beings and the powers possessed by a government created by those human beings:

> [T]he principal aim of society is to protect individuals in the enjoyment of those absolute rights, which were vested in them by the immutable laws of nature, but which could not be preserved in peace without that mutual assistance and intercourse which is gained by the institution of friendly and social communities. Hence it follows, that the first and primary end of human laws is to maintain and regulate these absolute rights of individuals. Such rights as are social and relative result from, and are posterior to, the formation of states and societies: so that to maintain and regulate these is clearly a subsequent consideration. And, therefore, the principal view of human laws is, or ought always to be, to explain, protect, and enforce such rights as are absolute...

Blackstone is certainly an authority of remarkable reputation, but let's move on to the clarity delivered through the application of another common analogy from contract law.

Imagine that a homebuilder and a future homeowner contract to build a house. A little while into the construction, the builder, without permission, begins digging a pool and charging the homeowner for those parts and the associated labor. Would the latter be obliged to pay those bills? Certainly not!

The man waiting for the house to be built would at first simply ignore the invoices, then if the builder insisted he be paid for the work on the pool, the future homeowner would simply refer to the terms of the contract as accepted by the builder and thus bind him to do only that work that was mutually agreed upon before work was ever begun.

Another aspect of contract law analogous to the search for legal justification of nullification is a subset of contract law — the law of agency.

The law of agency applies when one party gives another party legal authority to act on the first party's behalf. The first party is called the principal and the second party is called the agent. The principal may grant the agent as much or as little authority as suits his purpose. That is to say, by simply giving an agent certain powers, that agent is not authorized to act outside of that defined sphere of authority.

Upon its ratification, the states, as principals, gave limited power to the central government to act as their agent in certain matters of common concern: defense, taxation, interstate commerce, etc.

The authority of the agent — in this case the federal government — is derived from the agreement that created the principal/agent relationship. Whether the agent is lawfully acting on behalf of the principal is a question of fact. The agent may legally bind the principal only insofar as its actions lie within the contractual boundaries of its power. Should the agent exceed the scope of its authority, not only is the principal not held accountable for those acts, but the breaching agent is legally liable to the principal (and any affected third parties who acted in reliance on the agent's authority) for that breach.

As discussed above relating to contract law, under the law of agency, the principal may revoke the agent's authority at will. It would be unreasonable to oblige the principals to honor promises of an agent acting outside the boundaries of its authority as set out in the document that created the agency in the first place.

Imagine the chaos that would be created if principals were legally bound by the acts of an agent that "went rogue" and acted prejudicially to the interests of the principals from whom he derived any power in the first place. It is a fundamental tenet of the law of agency that the agent may lawfully act only for the benefit of the principal.

Inexplicably, this is the position taken by those who argue that the states may not nullify unconstitutional federal acts and refuse to be bound by an agent that repeatedly exceeds its authority. Not only does this agent (the federal government) habitually breach the agency contract, but it does so in a manner that irreparably harms the principal (the states).

To pull this down to the personal level again, imagine that a person's immense popularity puts him in a vulnerable position when he ventures out in public, so in order to avoid being swarmed by fans or assaulted by stalkers, the famous person hires a bodyguard to protect him from such harm.

Now imagine that every time the celebrity/employer leaves his house, the bodyguard/employee pummels his employer, leaving him weaker and more vulnerable than he was before he hired the bodyguard.

Do you think the famous person would continue paying the salary of the belligerent bodyguard?

More importantly, what would you think of the famous person if he did continue compensating the person he purportedly pays to protect him from harm?

How does it feel to realize that the states are the famous person/employer and the federal government is the bodyguard/employee and that we've put up with well over a century of being battered by the bodyguard and we pay him (the federal government) more and more every year, regardless of the perpetual pounding he puts us through?

Now, add to all this the fact that Congress is full of lawyers. Many presidents are lawyers. All federal judges are lawyers. Yet somehow when it comes to the relationship between the federal government and the states, they conveniently forget the basic principles of contract and agency law that are understood by second year law students.

You don't need a law degree, however, to understand that if the basic principles of the laws of contract and agency are applied to the relationship between states and general government as created in the Constitution the states' right of nullification becomes laughably simple and to borrow another phrase from Jefferson, "self evident."

Why do states not regularly assert these basic principles of contract and agency law? Perhaps it is because state legislators have been convinced — along with most of their constituents — that the federal government was created *ex nihilo* and the states are subordinate to its power.

Millions of Americans have learned in government-run schools and by experience after graduating that laws handed down from Capitol Hill are immutable, supreme, and must be obeyed by state legislatures, especially if they intend to retain their favorable positions at the federal trough. The flow of grant-in-aid funds would be stanched should a state presume to break the stick and throw the carrot back into the Potomac, ignoring all unconstitutional demands and dictates disguised as federal largesse.

The law and history are on our side. State delegates to the Constitutional Convention agreed upon the precise measure of their own governing authority they were granting to the federal government. The contract is the Constitution. The Constitution explicitly defines the limits of the federal government's powers and any power not granted to it by the states is retained by the states to be exercised according to **their** discretion and for **their** benefit.

It's right there in the contract.

Chapter 6

Nullification in Practice

SO, THE STATES CREATED the contract, the operation of which was the formation of a federal government. The federal government ignores that fact and acts under the assumption that citizens will do likewise. And so far, they've been right.

No longer.

Despite the frequent violations of the terms of the contract by the federal government, states are not left with the only option of voiding the contract. In fact, those state lawmakers and governors committed to forcing the federal beast back into its constitutional cage are better served by simply nullifying each and every congressional act or presidential decree that violates the agreed upon terms in the Constitution.

There are several benefits of this attitude: It preserves the union, demonstrates state allegiance to the principles of freedom that undergird the Constitution, and by extension, to our Founders.

Nullification is also preferable because it is a less radical reaction than secession. It is an ad hoc approach to ad hoc threats (acts that exceed the enumerated powers) that solves the sovereignty issue without dissolving the union.

That isn't to say, however, that secession should be taken off the table. No sovereign entity can by definition by compelled to continue association with any league, confederacy, or union that goes from being advantageous to despotic.

If, for example, a person joined a political party in order to help get people of a certain philosophical bent elected to office, there is nothing in reason or law that could compel that person to maintain membership in that party should that organization betray the fundamental principles which drew the person to the party in the beginning. The very premise is absurd.

Moreover, no matter how religiously devoted to the concept of the American union the people and their representatives may be, the fact remains that the commandment that there exist in perpetuity a United States of America was not etched into stone tablets on Mt. Sinai. If states decided that the federal authority has become destructive of the very ends it was created to protect, then it is the right of that state or states to — as someone once said of another formerly free government — "dissolve the political bands which have connected them with another, and to assume among the powers of the earth, the separate and equal station to which the Laws of Nature and of Nature's God entitle them...."

This principle was passionately and properly explained in 1848 by a little-known legislator from Illinois in a speech he delivered on the floor of the U.S. House of Representatives. Congressman Abraham Lincoln declared, regarding the right of the people to sever ties to a government they consider no longer acting in their best interest:

> Any people anywhere, being inclined and having the power, have the right to rise up and shake off the existing government, and form a new one that suits them better. This is a most valuable, a most sacred right—a right which, we hope and believe, is to liberate the world. Nor is this right confined to cases in which the whole people of an existing government may choose to exercise it. Any portion of such people that can may revolutionize, and make their own of so much of the territory as they inhabit. More than this, a majority of any portion of such people may revolutionize, putting down a minority, intermingled with, or near about them, who may oppose their movement.

How often did your high school history teacher read that speech to you during your discussion of the so-called "Civil War?" Didn't you learn that Lincoln was an ardent advocate of the "sacred right" of secession? Shocker.

The fact is that the laws of nature are immutable and cannot be altered simply by the assumption by one party power which does not legally appertain to it. It was so in 1776 and it is so now. Might does not make right.

The federal government may be stronger, richer, better armed, and possessed of monopolistic control of the press that prints all the money, but it is nevertheless has no right and no authority to impose its will on the states and the people, particularly when that will is set on aggrandizing itself to the detriment of those that gave it life.

With these facts in mind, let's look at two threshold questions that must be answered in order to decide whether nullification of a federal act is called for. First, does the act violate the Constitution's enumerated powers? Second, has every attempt at redress been made?

One very important fact must be stipulated to by the interested parties before setting about answering these questions. That fact is that the bodies constitutionally responsible for answering the two questions that precede a nullification of federal law are the state legislatures.

History, and our own experience, teaches us that once the muscle of tyranny develops in the body politic, it will never atrophy. The federal government has unconstitutionally assumed powers that do not pertain to it. They will continue to do so.

Every day, Congress, the president, and the judiciary will encroach farther and farther into the sovereign territory of the states. If the states appeal to the central government to police itself and restrain itself, then they must accept the response, which undoubtedly will constantly be for the states to mind their own business, the scope of which is continually shrinking.

Inevitably, there will be clashes when a state legislature begins batting around the idea of nullifying a federal act — don't believe for a second that the feds will just sit, roll over, or heel when they are commanded to do so. Although, when properly performed, nullification of unconstitutional federal acts is not necessarily confrontational.

There can be a pre-existing understanding between states and the federal government that states will not set in motion measures of secession or threaten revolution if the federal government, in turn, demonstrates its understanding that no act exceeding its constitutional boundaries will be given even the slightest, most perfunctory legal recognition by the states.

Additionally, if done right, nullification is a surgical, sparing way to remove malignant tumors of tyranny, not a chainsaw brutally butchering healthy and diseased tissue indiscriminately.

And, as I will discuss later, the road to redemption of state power would be even smoother were the 17th Amendment to be repealed making the Senate responsive and related to the state legislatures. After a time, a partnership would develop reducing the acrimony and fostering an understanding that any act of the central government exceeding the small sphere of power granted to it in the Constitution would be nullified.

What's the solution, then, to the winner-take-all mortal combat between the states and Washington? The routine and unrepentant nullification by the states of every unauthorized federal act. This practice would reduce, over time, the number and ferocity of the confrontations between Congress and state legislatures. As a bonus, the location of the clear boundaries of power will reappear from the dissipating fog of antagonism and autocracy.

There are those, however, who argue that there is a limit on the states' power of nullification. When the Supreme Court rules on the constitutionality of an act, however, nullification of that act is no longer an option.

In light of recent decisions by "conservatives" on the Supreme Court regarding the constitutionality of the Arizona immigration law and Obamacare, for example, it is no wonder that many Americans doubt that states maintain the right to nullify a congressional act after the Supreme Court has ruled on its constitutionality.

Thomas Jefferson had something to say in the matter. In 1804, he wrote that giving the Supreme Court power to declare unconstitutional acts of the legislature or executive "would make the judiciary a despotic branch." He noted that "nothing in the Constitution" gives the Supreme Court that right.

In this Mexican standoff of states, Supreme Court, and federal government, the last man standing is the people acting in their collective political capacity as states.

Even Abraham Lincoln, the old habeas corpus hater himself, recognized the lack of constitutional authority for the Supreme Court's assumption of the role of ultimate arbiter of an act's conformity with the Constitution.

Lincoln said that if the Supreme Court were afforded the power to declare whether on act of the federal government was constitutional, "the people will have ceased to be their own masters, having to that extent resigned their government into the hands of that eminent tribunal."

Consider also the opinion of imminent constitutional scholar, Von Holtz:

Moreover, violations of the Constitution may happen and the injured cannot, whether states or individuals, obtain justice through the court. Where the wrongs suffered are political in origin the remedies must be sought in a political way.

He continues, regarding this "aristocracy of the robe,": "That our national government, in any branch of it, is beyond the reach of the people; or has any sort of 'supremacy' except a limited measure of power granted by the supreme people is an error."

How can anyone read these statements, or the Tenth Amendment for that matter, and honestly conclude that any branch of the federal government is intended to be the surveyor of the boundaries of its own power? Every department of the federal government was created by the Constitution — therefore, by the states — and has no natural sovereignty. No branch can define its own authority. Such a thought is ridiculous and contrary to any theory of popular sovereignty ever enunciated. If courts, Congress, or presidents had such power, it would make them judge, jury, and executioner in every case in which their own act exceeding constitutional authority is at bar.

Look at it this way, if the federal government was "the decider" what purpose would the Tenth Amendment serve? Even the most sanguine political observer would admit that the federal government could, would, and does rule that every act is constitutional.

This is the case today and the consolidators genuinely believe that there is nothing they can't do, no law they can't pass, and no individual or government entity that can prevent them from enforcing those fiats masquerading as laws.

If we don't change our ways, soon we will learn that the loss of liberty is the worst of all possible fates and it always has and always will await the ignorant and the apathetic.

The failure of the people to force the states to flex the muscle of nullification has led to atrophy, leaving them too weak to put up a good fight against the federal assault on the sovereignty of the states and the liberty of the people.

As a result, Washington considers the states nothing more than administrative subordinates whose continued existence is tolerated only so long as they faithfully facilitate the execution of the millions of mandates of the multitude of federal programs.

The checks and balances of the Constitution and the separation of powers provided therein are meant to be the first layers of defense against tyranny, not the last or the only as the statists would have you believe. The people acting through their state governments are the final levee protecting the people as individuals from drowning under the flood of unconstitutional federal laws, regulations, and mandates.

States unwilling to be reduced to subordinates, subjects, and slaves must take as their motto: Sovereignty is not secession, rejection is not revolution, and nullification is not negation of the union.

Chapter 7

The Nullification Song: Solo or Chorus?

EVEN AMONG THOSE who espouse nullification as an answer to federal usurpations and encourage its practice by the states, though, there is an aspect of the states' power to reject unconstitutional federal acts that is rarely discussed.

This often overlooked element is that in the exercise of this exclusive authority, a state may unilaterally (that is, without the cooperation or agreement of any of her sister states or the permission of the federal government) nullify an act of Congress without assuming a revolutionary (secessionist) posture. If the other states decide not to nullify the measure found offensive by the nullifying state, neither the strength of the union nor the sovereignty of the non-nullifying states is diminished.

We need to re-learn this lesson and to reassert the sovereignty of the states we live in. We need to better understand that each state is absolutely sovereign and they have *never* surrendered that sovereignty. Accordingly, any one state or group of states may exercise that sovereignty by negating any unconstitutional act, regulation, or order of the general government — whether positively through acts of nullification or negatively through refusing to obey or enforce those acts.

Neither of those approaches to nullification requires a coalition of states to be effective. In fact, such a requirement of multi-state collaboration in this check on the general government usurpations would diminish the sovereignty of the individual state. Such a requirement would reduce the single state to temporary sovereign status, sovereign only in those instances when it agrees to join some provisional confederacy of other states opposing this or that act of the general government.

Ironically, perhaps, if a plurality (or a majority) of states nullified the same act or edict of one of the branches of the central government, the union would be strengthened by such a concerted commitment to the Constitution and the foundational principle of enumerated powers. Think of it this way: how much safer, cleaner, and attractive would a neighborhood be if the homeowners consistently enforced the terms of the covenant that created the Homeowners' Association? Federalism is a delicate flower that grows best when planted in the rich soil of constitutional consistency.

But that plot of land has lain fallow for so long and the weeds of centralism have grown so tall, that there are few legislators or laymen who remember the fertile, loamy soil that once nourished abundant acre upon abundant acre of the life-giving harvest of liberty.

Today, federalism is not only misunderstood, but misapplied by those who claim to appreciate its qualities.

For example, so often so-called "conservatives" will push back against the aggression of the federal government until the feds win (and they always do) and then the former foes retreat to safety behind the lines of the Supremacy Clause.

State legislators who consider themselves lawmakers per se, that is to say, not proxies for their colleagues on Capitol Hill, could foment real revolution without ever firing a shot and without ever filing a bill.

Nullification, whether exercised by one state or many, is a fact of constitutional construction and does not require a bill to trigger its protections of state sovereignty and individual liberty.

States who refuse to enforce an unconstitutional federal edict nullify that act just as positively and permanently as a state that proposes and passes a law negating that same measure.

After establishing a record of reliable resistance to attempts by the federal government to exercise unconstitutional powers, citizens of a state or states that effectively ignore the offending counterfeit law would learn in a generation or two that there are just some things that the federal government can't do. That state (or states) would gradually gain a gravitational pull, attracting men and women who value liberty above devotion to a "union" that has long since ceased to abide by the terms of the contract that created it and had grown so gargantuan as to prevent the justice and liberty it was organized to preserve.

Sadly, state lawmakers and governors have thus far failed to appreciate the right and responsibility they have to build these bulwarks of freedom. Perhaps more pragmatically relevant, they have failed to understand the amount of money that would be pumped into state budgets by a constant stream of immigrants (from within the union) seeking to be free from the crushing weight of federal mandates and monetary manipulation. When the first state assembly or the first state chief executive catches the vision of the viability and economic worth of a state where the Constitution is rigidly adhered to, there will be an immediate response by other states seeking to emulate that state's success. And nullification is the arm that will ring the bell, calling civil libertarians and constitutionalists to gather inside the borders of the bastions of liberty.

The Nullification Song: Solo or Chorus?

Until the dawn of the new day, it is curious that so many centralists and consolidationists deny the simplicity of the proposition that the general welfare is helped rather than hindered when a state government boldly asserts its right to judge the validity of acts of the federal government, for although all other states may disagree with the nullifying state's stance, the assumption thereof reinforces the remedy and its availability to all who feel the force of the federal boot on their neck.

In their support of the constitutionality of the application of the nullification doctrine by one state regardless of the posture of her sister states, the Kentucky and Virginia Resolutions are a "reaffirmation of the Spirit of 1776" as asserted by William J. Watkins in his book *Reclaiming the American Revolution*:

Whether made by one or many, these declarations of constitutional interpretations, like the Declaration of Independence, are statements renouncing the overreaching of government and reasserting the original right of other sovereignties to express that right and to require the central government to restrain itself within the sphere of power constitutionally assigned to it.

Watkins is right. It is important to recognize that the hand that wrote the Kentucky Resolutions also wrote the Declaration of Independence. Madison and Jefferson understood the wisdom of the proverb: "Start as you mean to go on." They likewise understood that even small and incremental deviations from the straight and narrow constitutional road would place this nation on a trajectory of tyranny — a path followed by so many of the formerly free governments of history.

Why do state legislators hesitate? Why do they deny the power that exists in them to put an end to the nearly constant contraction of liberty carried out by the federal government? Which state, if any, will become the site of the metaphorical Fort Sumter? Which governor, if any, will assert his constitutional prerogative to cut the cord from which dangles the federal carrot and break the stick over the knee of nullification?

One state. One state can lead the way. One state legislature can then take those sticks and rub them together until they spark a fire of freedom that will attract liberty-lovers to their borders like so many moths to the light of an irresistible flame.

Chapter 8

Principles of 1798 Solve the Problems of 2020

IN ORDER TO CHART a course toward the restoration of state sovereignty and constitutional principles of limited government, we don't need to look to the particular historical situation that prompted the drafting of the Virginia and Kentucky Resolutions. For our purposes, we benefit more from a study of the basic constitutional facts upon which these expressions of state resistance to federal tyranny are built. By drawing out of these wells of constitutional wisdom the timeless tenets of self-government that inform them, we may be able to effectively apply the Kentucky and Virginia Resolutions to our own unique contemporary constitutional challenges.

Jefferson and Madison knew that if the Constitution were to endure, state governments would have to steadfastly serve as barriers against the federal government's predictable assaults on liberty. In fact, it was the understanding that the Constitution, as proposed by the convention in Philadelphia in 1787, protected and preserved the power of the states to check any federal usurpation that convinced many fence-sitters during the ratification process to finally vote in favor of the new charter.

After reading the Kentucky and Virginia Resolutions, one wonders why in the last decade or so since the beginning of the undeclared but never ending "War on Terror," has there been no wholesale multi-state repudiation of warrantless wiretapping, warrantless pat downs at airports, warrantless death by drone, warrantless GPS tracking of cars, the near abolition of habeas corpus and codification of the indefinite detention of American citizens without due process of law.

Why have the states so completely and meekly abdicated their rightful position of power?

Why have they deserted their posts as sentinels set to watch for the approaching advance of federal absolutism?

Why do Americans look to Washington for cures to diseases bred by the swarms of would-be dictators that infest that former swamp?

Why do we sit idly by as congressmen, courts, and the president conspire to reduce our state governments to mere colonies of the federal empire?

Are state lawmakers and governors now so accustomed to their servitude that a benign stupor is their only reaction to the placement by the federal government of tighter and tighter chains around their necks?

Maybe we can find some answers to these troubling questions in the story of the prosecution of Samuel Jordan Cabell, one of the events that prompted Jefferson to pen the principles of nullification in 1798.

Cabell was a congressman representing Thomas Jefferson's home district in Virginia. In May 1797 a grand jury returned a presentment of libel against Cabell (incidentally, as a delegate to the Virginia ratifying convention, Cabell voted against ratification of the Constitution). What was Cabell's crime? He sent a letter to constituents criticizing the administration of John Adams. That's it. That was the sum of his seditious plot. A letter to voters in his district calling out some act of the president with which he disagreed.

For this effrontery to his authority, John Adams charged Cabell with "endeavoring at a time of real public danger to disseminate unfounded calumnies against the happy government of the United States...."

Sound familiar? How is it that an indictment sworn out by a jury over 200 years ago sounds like it could have been written yesterday? It's probably because we live in a time when the three branches of the federal government have managed to place themselves above reproach and above the law.

To help them reach that lofty perch, public schools and media have trained generations of Americans to believe that we must petition Washington for our salvation. If they ignore the plea, we must meekly accept the decision without question, especially when the Supreme Court rules that the federal position is now "settled law."

That was Samuel Jordan Cabell's predicament — caught in the spokes of a federal conspiracy — until Thomas Jefferson learned of the grand jury's action. In response to the presentment handed down against his congressman, Jefferson anonymously (for even the author of the Declaration of Independence feared being found openly questioning the national government) petitioned the Virginia House of Delegates asking that the members of the grand jury be punished.

Do we not see the sketch of a persecuted and frightened press in the story of Cabell? If a man as powerful, well-known, and well-regarded as Thomas Jefferson felt compelled to write under a pseudonym to avoid being hunted and hanged by agents of the federal government, is it any wonder that a Pulitzer Prize-winning journalist fears that his work with those labeled "enemy combatants" might get him thrown into a military prison for the duration of the "War on Terror?"

Consider the case of that journalist, Chris Hedges. Hedges is an award-winning foreign correspondent for the New York Times who fears a federal government empowered by an unconstitutional act to lock up those who dare challenge its authority.

Hedges (and a small group of other prominent writers, activists, and commentators) filed suit challenging the federal government's potential exercise of a provision in the National Defense Authorization Act (NDAA) that purports to authorize the indefinite detention of Americans suspected of aiding the enemy.

Although I'll examine it more thoroughly later, for now it is important only to understand that according to the text of Section 1021 of the Fiscal Year 2012 NDAA, the president may authorize the armed forces to indefinitely detain anyone he believes to have "substantially supported" al-Qaeda, the Taliban, or any unnamed "associated forces."

Fearing that this section could be applied to journalists and that the specter of such a scenario would have a chilling effect on free speech and freedom of the press in violation of the First Amendment, Hedges filed his lawsuit on January 12, 2012.

Hedges claims that his extensive work overseas, particularly in the Middle East, could qualify him as a "covered person" who, by way of such writings, interviews and/or communications, had "substantially supported" or "directly supported" "al-Qaeda, the Taliban or associated forces."

Such a classification, Hedges argues, could result in his being sent away indefinitely to a military detainment center without access to an attorney or habeas corpus relief.

Hedges would do well to look to Cabell's story as a presage of things to come.

Upon learning of Jefferson's petition in defense of Cabell, James Monroe counseled his fellow Virginian that he would be better off making his request to Congress instead of the state government. Jefferson's response makes it clear what the Sage of Monticello thought of Monroe's understanding of the true seat of sovereignty. He knew that "the system of the General Government is to seize all doubtful ground." If the people were to sit still, would we lose everything, he warned.

Who did Jefferson believe had the right and the responsibility to protect citizens from federal abuse of power? The states. "It is of immense consequence that the States retain as complete authority as possible over their own citizens," he wrote.

From this masterfully crafted letter in response to Monroe, we see that before he penned his views on the proper constitutional relationship between state and national government in the Kentucky Resolutions, Jefferson understood, shared, and promoted the principle of state authority to check federal overreaching.

If the states would perform their proper constitutional role as restated in the Kentucky and Virginia Resolutions, we wouldn't even speak of a state passing bills to nullify unconstitutional federal acts. Although such expressions of opposition are laudable, they are, constitutionally speaking, unnecessary. States have superior sovereignty and only have to negative federal usurpations by ignoring them. The fact that even patriots — those enlightened enough to understand the proper relationship between state and federal authority — push for passage of nullification bills demonstrates a latent inferiority complex that must be removed from the patriot psyche.

There is a fear associated with this feeling of inferiority. As I travel around the country speaking to constitutionalists and promoting this concept, I am routinely asked what would happen if a state were to actually ignore a federal mandate. "Wouldn't they send the army?" the listener routinely asks.

And I routinely answer: I don't know. Maybe federal troops would be deployed to the "rebellious" state to convince the obdurate state legislators to stand down and enforce the will of Washington or else.

All the wondering, all the musing, all the scenario concocting is academic. The fact is states don't take this tack. There hasn't been a single recent example of a state standing firm in its sovereign territory, unwilling to give quarter to the federal government.

Another question asked by well-meaning readers and listeners regarding the constitutionality of nullification and secession is: "Didn't the Civil War settle the issue of the right of secession?"

In a word: No. The Civil War made one thing clear: the federal government believes (and the Confederacy was forced to concede) that might makes right. The Union army defeated the army of the Confederacy, therefore, so the thinking goes, secession is no longer a constitutional remedy available to states. Might makes right.

Only it doesn't. Think of it this way. Assume my neighbor and I disagree over the exact location of the boundary line between our properties. One day, while I'm out building a shed that my neighbor believes encroaches on his property, we start arguing and the argument escalates to a full-fledged fist fight and I knock out my neighbor. Does that mean that the location of our mutual property line has been settled? Does the pummeling of my neighbor make my opinion of the location of that line the legal boundary? Of course not. Might, it seems, does not make right, neither in boundary disputes regarding land nor in similar conflicts over state sovereignty.

Nullification, as defined by Jefferson and Madison, is the most powerful weapon against the federal assault on state sovereignty and individual liberty. By applying the principles put forth in those seminal documents, states can simultaneously rebuild the walls of sovereignty once protected by the Constitution, in particular the Tenth Amendment, and drive the forces of federal consolidation back to the banks of the Potomac.

Returning to the weather analogy, in the face of the downpour of federal despotism, states shouldn't waste time opening the umbrella of non-binding resolutions when they have the constitutionally protected power to stop (nullify) the rain?

Chapter 9

Immigration Versus Naturalization

IN THIS SECTION, we'll look at a few of the current constitutional issues that could (and should) be settled permanently by nullification. First up is immigration.

As with so many things that are true and constitutionally accurate, here's something you don't read very often in the media, online, or hear from the floor of Congress: Congress has no enumerated power over immigration.

That's right, the Constitution grants none of the branches of the federal government any power over immigration. Article I, Section 8 invests Congress with authority over the establishment of "rules of naturalization."

Again, as we saw with the understanding of nullification, there was a time in our nation's history when this wasn't such a difficult distinction to grasp.

During deliberation of the Civil War amendments (13th and 14th), Ulysses S. Grant recognized that immigration was a state issue and not merely an aspect of naturalization. In a memo to the House of Representatives, Grant wrote:

Responsibility over immigration can only belong with the States since this is where the Constitution kept the power.

In order to better illustrate the relationship of immigration to naturalization, here comes another analogy from everyday life.

Consider love and marriage for a minute. The government doesn't require a license to get engaged and it takes no part in overseeing the break-up of engaged people. Men and women are free to enter and end engagements without any interference from the government.

If the engagement lasts, however, and the happy couple wants to make it permanent, they must conform to certain legal requirements established by state governments. They must apply for a license, then wait a statutorily prescribed time between obtaining the license and solemnizing the ceremony. Typically, they also must affirm that they are not already married, that they are of legal age, etc.

This process is comparable to the one undertaken by an immigrant in order to become a citizen.

Imagine the chaos that would ensue if the government were to insinuate itself into the business of approval of getting engaged, staying engaged, and breaking off an engagement. As unlikely as this seems, this is exactly the situation that occurs when the federal government tries to monitor and control the flow of immigrants into the 50 states.

In what is a very familiar story, the Obama administration perpetuated the myth of federal exclusivity over immigration by filing a federal lawsuit challenging the constitutionality of S.B. 1070, a bill lawfully passed by the Arizona legislature and signed into law by Governor Jan Brewer.

In June, 2012, the Supreme Court issued its ruling on the case against Arizona's immigration statute. In the decision, one of the four provisions at issue was upheld, while the remaining three were struck down.

The part of the law upheld by the justices is that permitting law enforcement to verify the immigration status of anyone even briefly detained as a part of a routine stop.

The justices struck down the three remaining provisions of S.B. 1070 that were up for review. Those three parts of the law are:

• Making it a crime for an illegal immigrant to work or to seek work in Arizona;

• Authorizing state and local law enforcement to arrest a suspect without a warrant if the officers can show probable cause to believe that the suspect is illegally present in the state; and

• Mandating that all immigrants register with the federal government.

On behalf of the majority, Justice Kennedy wrote:

The National Government has significant power to regulate immigration. With power comes responsibility, and the sound exercise of national power over immigration depends on the Nation's meeting its responsibility to base its laws on a political will informed by searching, thoughtful, rational civic discourse. Arizona may have understandable frustrations with the problems caused by illegal immigration while that process continues, but the State may not pursue policies that undermine federal law.

Despite this despicable and inexplicable misreading of the Constitution, there was someone on that bench speaking sense. In a dissenting opinion replete with references to the sovereignty of the states, Justice Scalia wrote:

Today's opinion, approving virtually all of the Ninth Circuit's injunction against enforcement of the four challenged provisions of Arizona's law, deprives States of what most would consider the defining characteristic of sovereignty: the power to exclude from the sovereign's territory people who have no right to be there. Neither the Constitution itself nor even any law passed by Congress supports this result.

In his dissenting opinion, Scalia strikes a very constitutional chord, repeatedly reminding the Court that the United States is a creation of the states and that as such it was granted only that authority specifically enumerated in the Constitution. Scalia wrote:

> There is no doubt that "before the adoption of the constitution of the United States" each State had the authority to "prevent [itself] from being burdened by an influx of Persons...." And the Constitution did not strip the States of that authority. To the contrary, two of the Constitution's provisions were designed to enable the States to prevent "the intrusion of obnoxious aliens through other States." Letter from James Madison to Edmund Randolph (Aug. 27, 1782).

Then, questioning whether the United States would ever have been created given the impact of today's ruling. Justice Scalia wondered whether the states would even have formed the union had they realized that one day they would be "at the mercy of the Federal Executive's refusal to enforce the Nation's immigration laws."

Finally, in his own inimical way, Justice Scalia puts a finely honed point on his argument against striking down S.B. 1070: "If securing its territory in this fashion is not within the power of Arizona, we should cease referring to it as a sovereign State."

Amen.

Justice Scalia, as he so often is, was spot on. For no matter the accumulation of judicial decisions or federal lawsuits, the fact is that the Constitution of the United States nowhere grants the national government the exclusive (or even concurrent, for that matter) authority to regulate matters of immigration.

The closest the Constitution comes to placing anything even incidentally related to immigration within the realm of Congressional authority is found in the clause of Article I, Section 8 that empowers Congress to "establish a uniform Rule of Naturalization." That's it. There is no other mention of immigration in the text of the Constitution. Somehow, though, the enemies of the right of states to govern themselves have extrapolated from that scant reference to "naturalization" the exclusive right of Congress to legislate in the arena of immigration.

The difference between immigration and naturalization is clearly defined in the law — both before and after the passage of the 14th Amendment. Immigration is the act of coming to a country of which one is not a native. Naturalization, however, is defined as the conference upon an alien of the rights and privileges of a citizen. It is difficult to understand how so many lawyers, judges, and legislators (most of whom are or were lawyers) can consistently confuse these two words.

Did the founders misunderstand these terms, as well? Let's look to history for a little enlightenment.

Before they sent delegates to a convention in Philadelphia in 1787 to amend the Articles of Confederation, states were already regulating immigration by setting rules governing the means by which people could lawfully enter. Put another way, they were policing the immigration of aliens, an act all of them understood to be within their rights as a sovereign government.

So universal was this understanding that not once during that summer of 1787 did any one of the fifty-five (on and off) representatives of the 13 states suggest that the states should surrender power to regulate immigration to the new federal government. That is significant. Not even the most strident advocate of a powerful national government ever proposed granting the power in question to the central authority.

In fact, the sole reference to the federal government's power to regulate immigration is Article I, Section 9 wherein Constitution forbids Congress from interfering in the "migration or importation" of persons into the several states until 1808. That this limitation concerned the slave trade and only the slave trade is patently obvious to anyone reading the debates of the convention as recorded by James Madison and others who were present at the time. In fact, the wording of Article I, Section 9 is purposefully worded as it is so as not to be confused with any other article of the Constitution.

During the process of considering specific bills aimed at carrying out the enumerated power of setting the rules of naturalization, several Congressmen spoke on the record about the proper constitutional boundaries meant to encompass congressional action in this regard.

In an excellent article written by Vincent Gioia, the statements of several congressmen are recounted, all of which point to the general understanding that immigration was a state matter, with power over the establishment of rules for naturalization given to the federal government.

Gioia quotes one congressman saying during the debate on the 14th Amendment, "All, therefore, that the House have to do on this subject, is to confine themselves to an uniform rule of naturalization and not to a general definition of what constitutes the rights of citizenship in the several States."

With all this in mind, it is a curious thing to consider how so many congressmen, trained in the law generally and in the interpretation of the Constitution specifically, could wholly and habitually misread the plain language of that document, unless that was their intent.

Surely, these elected representatives know that not a single pen stroke was made on that parchment granting Congress the power to control immigration. The silence of the Constitution on this matter, as well as the legislative history of the laws enacted to carry out the related enumerated powers, reveals the founders intended for the states to retain the plenary power over immigration. This includes the right to decide who may or may not pass through their borders or reside within them.

Chapter 10

Severing The Tie That Bound State And Senate

THE 17TH AMENDMENT is one of the changes that has most significantly altered the Constitution as originally agreed to by the states. As drafted and approved, the Senate was to be the tether connecting Congress to the state legislatures.

As is the case with the immigration, there are a few legislators who then and now understand and appreciate the apparently irreparable harm done to the Constitution and to federalism by the ratification of the 17th Amendment. One of those well-informed lawmakers is former U.S. Senator Zell Miller.

On April 28, 2004, Miller stood on the floor of the Senate and introduced Joint Resolution 35, a bill to repeal the 17th Amendment to the Constitution. In the statement accompanying the introduction of his bill, Senator Miller said, "The election of Senators by the State legislatures was the lynchpin that guaranteed the interests of the States would be protected."

He further explained that ratification of the 17th Amendment was "a victory for special-interest tyranny and a blow to the power of State governments that would cripple them forever."

Although the enemies of freedom and constitutional good government are running the show and setting the agenda when it comes to protecting the 17th Amendment, it wasn't always so. In the early years of our nation, many of our most illustrious founders regarded and promoted federalism as one of America's first and foremost principles.

Edmund Randolph, governor of Virginia and representative of that state at the Constitutional Convention, said that the object of the particular mode of electing senators was "to control the democratic branch." Recognizing the terrors historically accompanying any government possessed by the demon of democracy, Randolph believed that "a firmness and independence may be the more necessary in this branch, as it ought to guard the Constitution against encroachments of the Executive who will be apt to form combinations with the demagogues of the popular branch."

James Madison echoed his fellow Virginian's sentiment, declaring, "the use of the Senate is to consist in its proceeding with more coolness, with more system, and more wisdom than the popular branch" and to "protect the people against the transient impressions in which they themselves might be led...."

During the debates on the subject in the Convention, Luther Martin of Maryland described it bluntly and accurately: "The Senate is to represent the states."

Finally, Roger Sherman, an influential delegate to the Constitutional Convention of 1787, wrote in a letter to John Adams: "The senators, being . . . dependent on [state legislatures] for reelection, will be vigilant in supporting their rights against infringement by the legislative or executive of the United States."

With Sherman's assessment in mind, it is reasonable to regard the abolition of this check on the legislative and executive branches of the central government as a tactic of the enemies of the Constitution. With the "artillery" of state legislatures silenced by the 17th Amendment, then, the ability of the legislative and executive branches of the federal government to consolidate all power into their hands is exponentially increased. Indeed, the sprawling tree of federal supremacy was planted, took root, grew, and thrived in the post-17th Amendment electoral environment.

Tragically, the fruit of this poisonous tree has been swallowed by so many that most people believe it is a native American plant. In fact, if polled, it is likely that most Americans would express a preference for continuing on with the post-17th Amendment scheme of representation.

Given this constant diet of misinformation, it isn't difficult to forgive most Americans for not recognizing that a fundamental principle of federalism is violated by the failure to repeal the 17th Amendment. In fairness, for generations Americans have been force fed this tripe by a government that has been unlawfully afforded superintendence over the education of the nation's children.

The words of the Founders rehearsed earlier in the chapter are a solid foundation upon which to build our understanding of the miracle that the structure of our Constitution. We should look with awe and appreciation on the remarkable and inimitable Constitution drafted by our Founders. As part of this, we should add the knowledge that these men spent countless hours in the laboratory of self-government working out the most stable composition of a republican and federal system of government.

The specific ingredients in the American Experiment were very carefully chosen and precisely measured by the political scientists that took the lead in founding our republic. The concoction they cooked up proved both stable and potent. Students of this grand endeavor must be warned that fiddling with that formula, especially by those not as well versed in the history of the disastrous outcomes of other similar experiments by statesmen of the past, will have predictable and pernicious results.

That said, there remains a very widespread concern that a return to the original, pre-17th Amendment construction of the Constitution would deny citizens of a state the right to elect their representatives? My answer: Yes and no.

Let me begin the process of chopping at the tree of misinformation by rehearsing a little of the history of the problem.

The 17th Amendment to the United States Constitution was ratified in 1913 and reads in relevant part: "The Senate of the United States shall be composed of two Senators from each State, elected by the people thereof...." As set forth in the original text of Article 1, senators were to be "chosen by the Legislature" of the states. Inarguably, then, the 17th Amendment stripped the state legislatures of their right and responsibility to elect senators to the federal government and gave it to the people.

Remember, the federal legislative branch was not designed as a parliament of representatives of the people, but as a congress – a bicameral assembly of representatives of the people and representatives of the sovereign states. It was designed as an amalgamation of the two authorities whose measured cession of sovereignty created the national government.

In the Senate, it was not "the people's" interests that were meant to be advocated in this arrangement. That role, the role of representing the will of the people at large, was given to the House of Representatives.

Even schoolchildren are taught that the framers of the Constitution of the United States created a federal government of separated powers that should check and balance each other. While establishing a dynamic and robust central authority, the Founding Fathers in their wisdom tempered the natural tendency of such a government to accumulate authority by relying upon the equally sovereign states and the retardant effect they would have upon this tendency of consolidated governments to grow unwieldy and tyrannical.

To that end, on Thursday, June 7, 1787, the delegates to the Constitutional Convention voted unanimously to grant the seasoned and popularly elected representatives in the various state legislatures the power to elect members of the national senate. The river of representation of the people was to be distilled through several layers of elected representation (the definition of federalism). The people were to be represented in the new senate as citizens of the states. Thus, removed as it was by degrees from the heat and mercurial temperament of the momentary passions of the people, said Edmund Randolph, the Senate would act as a check against the "turbulence and follies of democracy."

The ratification of the 17th Amendment deprived the nation of this crucial counterbalance. This gave full rein to the aggressive accumulation of power that comes from the destructive devices that are the means and ends of the combination of demagogues that for decades have populated the executive and legislative branches.

All that work at the Constitutional Convention notwithstanding, on April 8, 1913, that check has been abolished and the nation was pushed closer toward falling into the one of the innumerable deadly chasms of democracy. The senate no longer reflects the political philosophy of our Founding Fathers that the states were best suited to respond to the legitimate needs of their citizens.

Designing centralists sacrificed the interests of the "United States" on the altar of popular democracy. Sadly, our Founders knew that all the republics of history died on that altar and they, through the mechanism of federalism and states rights, sought to save the confederation they were forming from this violent fate.

Chapter 11

The National Defense Authorization Act (NDAA)

O N WEDNESDAY, JANUARY 2, 2013, President Barack Obama did what constitutionalists and civil libertarians knew he would do: He signed into law the renewal of his power to apprehend and detain Americans indefinitely on no more authority than his own suspicion of their complicity with enemies in the "War on Terror."

With more of a whimper than a bang, the president signed the Fiscal Year 2013 National Defense Authorization Act (NDAA). As he did on New Year's Eve 2011 when he signed last year's version of the NDAA, President Obama appended a signing statement to the act. This time, however, there were no promises of protecting Americans from deprivations of due process. This time, the signing statement (I would agree with Benjamin Wittes of the Lawfare blog who suggests it is more of a "whining" statement) recounts all the reasons the president had for vetoing the bill.

Somehow, however, he managed to hold his nose and sign this unconstitutional, no longer unprecedented, giant leap toward statism, absolutism, and outright unapologetic tyranny.

Although President Obama warned months ago that he would veto the $636-billion defense spending bill if it contained any restrictions on his ability to shutter the detention facility at Guantanamo Bay, Cuba (a 2008 campaign promise), he apparently decided that compared to the power to kidnap and lock up Americans according to his own whim was sufficient exchange for being "forced" to keep Gitmo going.

Leaders of human rights organizations — many of whom were counted among the winning Obama coalition in 2008 — admitted disappointment at the failure of the president to deliver the hope and change he promised.

"It's not encouraging that the President continues to be willing to tie his own hands when it comes to closing Guantanamo," said Dixon Osburn of Human

Rights First. "The injustice of Guantanamo continues to serve as a stain on American global leadership on human rights."

Frank Jannuzi, deputy executive director of Amnesty International USA said that "solutions for ending human rights violations, not excuses, must be found."

"This law makes it harder for the President to fulfill his promise to close the Guantanamo detention facility, perpetuating a grave injustice against the detainees held without charge or fair trial," Jannuzi added.

Fair trials are likely to soon be placed on the federally protected endangered species list.

There were a few lawmakers, however, who tried to amend the NDAA in a way that protected that fundamental right for Americans or permanent legal residents detained under provisions of the NDAA.

On December 18, 2012 the House and Senate Armed Services Committees completed their conference report on the National Defense Authorization Act (NDAA) for Fiscal Year 2013. This was the version of the bill signed by President Obama on January 2, 2013.

At a press conference held December 20, 2012 four of the leaders of those committees announced the completion of the compromise version of the bill and pointed out some highlights of the revised bicameral measure.

"The conference report on the National Defense Authorization Act for Fiscal Year 2013, which was adopted today by the conference committee, provides well-deserved support for the men and women of the armed forces and their families and provides them with the means to accomplish their missions," announced Senator Carl Levin (D-Mich.).

One controversial portion of the NDAA bill passed by the Senate on December 4, 2012 didn't make the cut, however, after the conference committee's negotiations.

The Feinstein-Lee Amendment, which protects Americans from indefinite detention (passed by the Senate 67-29), was stripped from the conference report, not surprising given that inveterate warmonger Senator John McCain (R-Ariz.) led the group drafting the compromise version of the bill that would be presented to both houses for their approval.

The relationship between McCain's influence and the exclusion of the Feinstein-Lee Amendment from the conference report was not lost on Senator Rand Paul (R-Ky.), a chief co-sponsor of the Feinstein-Lee Amendment.

In a statement released on December 19, 2012 Senator Paul did what few lawmakers ever do — he named names:

The decision by the NDAA conference committee, led by Sen. John

McCain (R-Ariz.) to strip the National Defense Authorization Act of the amendment that protects American citizens against indefinite detention now renders the entire NDAA unconstitutional.

Later in the speech, Senator Paul equates voting for the NDAA to a violation of the oath of office taken by every senator.

Members of the House of Representatives were right there with their congressional colleagues in faithlessness to their oaths of office.

In a shameful display of disregard for the Constitution and for liberty, on May 18, 2012, the House of Representatives overwhelmingly voted to perpetuate the president's power to indefinitely detain American citizens.

By a vote of 238-182, members of Congress rejected an amendment offered by Representatives Adam Smith (D-Wash.) and Justin Amash (R-Mich.) that would have repealed the indefinite detention provision passed overwhelmingly last year as part of the National Defense Authorization Act of 2012.

The Fiscal Year 2013 NDAA retained the indefinite detention provisions, as well as the section permitting prisoners to be transferred from civilian jurisdiction to the custody of the military.

During House debate on the issue, Representative Amash said:

The frightening thing here is that the government is claiming the power under the Afghanistan authorization for use of military force as a justification for entering American homes to grab people, indefinitely detain them and not give them a charge or trial.

In his impassioned speech supporting his amendment, Representative Smith reminded his colleagues that the NDAA granted to the president "extraordinary" powers and divested the American people of key civil liberties, as well as divesting civilian courts of their constitutional jurisdiction.

Smith pointed out that there was no need to transfer suspects into military custody, as "hundreds" of terrorists have been tried in federal courts since the attacks of September 11, 2001.

Congressmen — Republicans and Democrats — were not persuaded and they voted down the Smith-Amash amendment.

Another amendment offered by Representatives Louie Gohmert (R-Texas), Jeff Landry (R-La.), and Scott Rigell (R-Va.) passed by a vote of 243-173. The Gohmert Amendment (House Amendment 1126) states that the NDAA will not "deny the writ of habeas corpus or deny any Constitutional rights for persons detained in the United States under the AUMF who are entitled to such rights."

Again, this amendment is yet another indefensible use of vague language that would make it vulnerable to challenge in any court in any state in the Union, but somehow adds to its appeal among the Republicans in Congress.

Section 1029 of the 2013 NDAA purports to protect the rights of citizens, relying again on lazy language that would fail a legal challenge if it were a city ordinance and not a congressional act.

That section declares:

Nothing in the Authorization for Use of Military Force (Public Law 107-40; 50 U.S.C. 1541 note) or the National Defense Authorization Act for Fiscal Year 2012 (Public Law 112-81) shall be construed to deny the availability of the writ of habeas corpus or to deny any Constitutional rights in a court ordained or established by or under Article III of the Constitution to any person inside the United States who would be entitled to the availability of such writ or to such rights in the absence of such laws.

Not surprisingly, this brief paragraph fails to address the most invasive aspect of the mortal malady that is the NDAA — the placement of the American military at the disposal of the president for the apprehension, arrest, and detention of those suspected of posing a danger to the homeland (whether inside or outside the borders of the United States and whether the suspect be a citizen or foreigner). Giving the president that power is nothing less than a de facto legislative repeal of the Posse Comitatus Act of 1878, the law forbidding the use of the military in domestic law enforcement.

Stalinist-style authoritarianism is the NDAA's true threat to liberty. While Section 1029 purports to buttress the right to a trial for citizens and permanent residents, it does nothing to prevent their apprehension. Denial of habeas corpus (or a trial) comes later; it is the delirium, not the fever, in a manner of speaking.

The bottom line is Americans would not need to worry about being held without charge if the president was not authorized in the same act to deploy the armed forces to round up the "suspects" and detain them indefinitely. Being apprised of the laws one is accused of having violated is important, but it's the detention and the manner of it that must be of more immediate concern to those who are alarmed about the new world order being defined by the NDAA.

Since the beginning of hostilities in the wake of 9/11, the federal government has often had problems proving membership in al-Qaeda of those arrested as "enemy combatants" in the War on Terror, so imagine the difficulty they would face in presenting evidence of affiliation or adherence to that shadowy, ill-defined organization.

The danger of the vagueness of crucial terms of the NDAA was addressed by Congressman Ron Paul (R-Texas) during a phone conference with supporters in Iowa:

> The dangers in the NDAA are its alarmingly vague, undefined criteria for who can be indefinitely detained by the US government without trial. It is now no longer limited to members of al Qaeda or the Taliban, but anyone accused of "substantially supporting" such groups or "associated forces." How closely associated? And what constitutes "substantial" support? What if it was discovered that someone who committed a terrorist act was once involved with a charity? Or supported a political candidate? Are all donors of that charity or supporters of that candidate now suspect, and subject to indefinite detainment? Is that charity now an associated force?

Fortunately for the President, the NDAA absolves him of the requirement of gathering and presenting to an impartial judge evidence probative of such evil associations. The mere suspicion of such suffices as a justification for the indefinite imprisonment of those so suspected.

As if the foregoing wasn't an imposing enough threat to freedom, there is an additional aspect of the NDAA that places the civil liberties of Americans in greater peril.

The undeniable unconstitutionality of the National Defense Authorization Act and its violation of the Posse Comitatus Act increases the urgency for states to nullify those sections of the law that exceed the enumerated powers of Congress. This remedy would be applied by the legislatures of the states in an effort to protect its citizens from arrest and extradition by members of the federal armed forces. This effort to resist unfettered federal authority would rival the intensity of the Nullification Crisis of the 1830s — a confrontation that culminated in the Civil War and the death of at least 600,000 Americans.

While the frightening abolition of civil liberties contained in the NDAA could not have been codified were it not for the signature of President Obama, the complicity of the Congress in easing our republic's "slip into tyranny" should not be overlooked. Nearly 70 percent of our "elected representatives" in Congress voted in favor of the NDAA in 2012 and year after year the overwhelming majority of congressmen continue to give the greenlight to this unconscionable and unconstitutional denial of some of the most basic civil and natural rights.

With the annual renewal of the NDAA, the depth of the impact of this law on the freedom of Americans and the perpetuation of our Constitution cannot be measured. Promises to restrain oneself from abusing power are unreliable. As Thomas Jefferson once warned:

> Free government is founded in jealousy, not confidence. It is jealousy

and not confidence which prescribes limited constitutions, to bind those we are obliged to trust with power.... In questions of power, then, let no more be heard of confidence in men, but bind him down from mischief by the chains of the Constitution.

Thankfully, constitutionally aware state legislators and citizens are repairing the walls of state sovereignty, proposing and passing state measures nullifying the provisions of the NDAA most noxious to civil liberty.

States whose legislatures are enlightened and emboldened enough to pass laws nullifying the NDAA will become refuges for citizens fleeing a federal government that has for years behaved as an enemy of freedom.

Finally, the embarrassing distinction between those who lived under and labored to repeal the Alien and Sedition Acts and those of use who live under the NDAA is that as agents of the John Adams administration roamed the country enforcing the gag order, "remonstrances and resolutions" issued from every district in every state "bearing tens of thousands of names" and were delivered daily to the very halls of Congress.

How many letters, emails, or phone calls are received by Congress remonstrating against the passage of the NDAA? Sure there are some, but would anyone seriously suggest that they would amount to anything close to "tens of thousands?" And given the population of the United States today compared to what it was in 1798, the letters should proportionally number in the tens of millions. Not even close.

Chapter 12

Obamacare

WE'RE ALL FAMILIAR WITH the classic shell game. We follow the ball. We know the huckster's tricks and we know he is moving it around to trip us up, but we believe our eyes are faster than the huckster's hands.

Since the day in November 2011 when the Supreme Court announced that it would hear the ObamaCare case, Americans watched the ball of the individual mandate. We reckoned that we knew where the huckster was going to put it and some of us thought there was even a chance that it would fall off the table completely.

Then in June 2012, after we all had placed our bets, confident that it would show up under the Commerce Clause shell, the huckster ended the game by revealing the location of the individual mandate ball: It was under the Taxation Clause shell. We all guessed wrong and we all lost.

Perhaps the strangest part of last year's Supreme Court ruling upholding the constitutionality of ObamaCare was the reasoning relied on by Chief Justice John Roberts to justify the decision.

In plain language, Roberts said that although the government cannot force you to buy a commodity (health insurance), it can tax you if you don't.

Then, so no one will misunderstand exactly what will now be required under ObamaCare, the Court declared: "The most straightforward reading of the individual mandate is that it commands individuals to purchase insurance." Your federal overlords now command you to purchase a qualifying healthcare plan and will impose an additional tax should you refuse to obey.

In a fair reading of the decision, the Supreme Court says that the penalty for failure to purchase healthcare insurance is not a tax for the purpose of the application of the Anti-Injunction Act, but it is a tax for the purpose of interpreting the taxing power of the Constitution. The relevant portion of the majority opinion reads:

The Affordable Care Act describes the payment as a "penalty," not a "tax." That label cannot control whether the payment is a tax for purposes of the Constitution, but it does determine the application of the Anti-Injunction Act. The Anti-Injunction Act therefore does not bar this suit.

The reasoning upholding the individual mandate as a tax expressly contradicts President Obama's public defense of his pet legislation. In an interview with George Stephanopoulos of ABC News in 2009, President Obama adamantly denied that the individual mandate was a tax. "I absolutely reject that notion," the President said.

Given the fact that the Affordable Care Act explicitly states that the individual mandate penalty is not a tax and that its proponents universally defended the provision on that same ground, what Chief Justice John Roberts did amounts to no more or less than scrapping ObamaCare and giving us RobertsCare.

Despite the government's attorneys arguing that the individual mandate is a penalty and not a tax (as President Obama told Stephanopoulos), Roberts dismissed the administration's label, declaring that the penalty was a tax and therefore permissible under Article I, Section 8 of the Constitution.

Despite the distinction and the Roberts re-write, the President won't quibble over the labels. A penalty or a tax, ObamaCare is unconstitutional regardless of how many black-robed tyrants say otherwise.

The Obamacare decision is judicial activism at its finest. The Supreme Court was so determined to endow the federal government with unlimited power and to toss the notion of enumerated powers onto the scrap heap of history that it was willing to effect a fundamental change to the law as enacted by Congress and the President.

In the Obamacare ruling, the Supreme Court not only re-wrote ObamaCare, but it simultaneously united the power of making and interpreting law into their own unelected hands.

As it stands now, the people's representatives may presume to pass laws in accordance with their constitutionally enumerated powers, but if the Supreme Court wishes to rubber stamp the president's pronouncements and afford them the power of law, the justices will simply substitute language permitting any imaginable act of despotism in open defiance of any congressional intent to the contrary.

The Obamacare ruling is a perfect example of the situation described by Patrick Henry during the Virginia ratification convention when Congress and the courts collude to rob states of sovereignty and citizens of liberty. Said Henry:

If there be a real check intended to be left on Congress, it must be left in the state governments. There will be some check, as long as the judges are incorrupt. As long as they are upright, you may preserve your liberty. But what will the judges determine when the state and federal authority come to be contrasted? Will your liberty then be secure, when the congressional laws are declared paramount to the laws of your state, and the judges are sworn to support them?

In addition to the individual mandate forcing Americans to buy a good or commodity (health insurance), there are even more frightening aspects of ObamaCare empowering the federal government to force us to live according to how the government decides best.

For example, the much-maligned "death panels" are now the law; federal funding for abortion is now the law; the reduction of states to mere vassals of the federal emperor is now law. As John Birch Society CEO Art Thompson said, the federal government now "will intrude on every aspect of life in America, from cradle to grave."

And most importantly, Washington may now decide who makes it to the cradle and who gets pushed into the grave.

Not a single one of our Founding Fathers, not even the most ardent advocate of a powerful central government, would have remained a single day at the Philadelphia Convention if they believed that the government they were creating would become the instrument of tyranny that it has become.

The saddest fact, however, is that not only has Congress passed unconstitutional laws, the president issued despotic edicts, and the Courts upheld every unimaginable expansion of federal power, but the states have obeyed these orders.

They may occasionally pull at the leash or nip at the hand that feeds them, but they slaver over the scraps tossed to them by their federal masters.

As the states have become servants, they may yet regain their proper role as masters. In this there is hope, in fact.

The states, through the exercise of the Tenth Amendment and their natural right to rule as sovereign entities, may stop ObamaCare at the state borders by enacting state statutes nullifying the healthcare law and criminalizing state participation in administering or executing the unconstitutional provisions thereof.

Nullification is the "rightful remedy" and is a much more constitutionally sound method of checking federal usurpation and is quicker and less complicated than an attempt to have the law repealed by Congress or overturned by a future federal bench more respectful of the Constitution. That said, there is no reason that concerned citizens should not use every weapon in the Constitutional arsenal, including working to convince Congress to repeal this offensive act.

What Degree Of Madness

The Supreme Court's ratification of ObamaCare's individual mandate can be seen as a mandate of another sort. Americans should now turn their attention to removing from office every congressman who voted in favor of the "law" and electing those candidates for state legislature who will commit themselves to boldly asserting the sovereignty of the states and forcing the raging bull of the federal government back within the small and well-defined corral built by our Founding Fathers.

As the multitude of unconstitutional mandates contained within the ObamaCare behemoth begin breathing down the necks of Americans, thankfully, there are a few state legislators proposing bills to protect citizens from being subjected to the healthcare law.

Legislatures in many states have considered or are considering bills or resolutions aimed at defying the Obamacare mandates within the borders of their respective states.

The growth of this movement is not only encouraging, but evidence of a increase in state assemblies of the proper role of states in checking the federal government.

Perhaps most demoralizing is the fact that for years the Congress and the White House were controlled by Republicans, a party that ran on a promise to "repeal Obamacare" as soon as a president from the GOP was elected.

In 2016, Donald Trump was elected — to the surprise of many — and he, too, promised his millions of supporters that he would undo ObamaCare and all of its unconstitutional assaults on the freedom and the finances of the American people.

Has President Trump fulfilled that campaign promise?

No.

In fact, on June 24, 2019 President Trump issued an executive order entitled "Executive Order on Improving Price and Quality Transparency in American Healthcare to Put Patients First," declaring that "by the authority vested in [him] as President by the Constitution," he was going "to enhance the ability of patients to choose the healthcare that is best for them."

In remarks made at the White House announcing the issuing of the order, the president made it clear just how much power he presumes he has:

> We're here to announce new groundbreaking actions that we're taking to dramatically increase quality, affordability, and fairness to our healthcare system. This landmark initiative continues our campaign to put American patients first. This is a truly big action. People have no idea how big it is. Some people say bigger than healthcare itself. This is something that's going to be very important.

Read that again. President Trump signed an executive order giving the federal government control over healthcare to such a scope that the federal government's control over healthcare is now "bigger than healthcare itself."

That should be shocking, but the language of the edict is even more expansive.

The president's proclamation declared that it "is the policy of the Federal Government to ensure that patients are engaged with their healthcare decisions and have the information requisite for choosing the healthcare they want and need."

Additionally, the president insisted in his diktat that it is also the responsibility of the federal government to "eliminate unnecessary barriers to price and quality transparency; to increase the availability of meaningful price and quality information for patients; to enhance patients' control over their own healthcare resources, including through tax-preferred medical accounts; and to protect patients from surprise medical bills."

Other than an oblique reference to the "authority vested in" him by the Constitution, President Trump did not point to the precise provision of the Constitution where the states that ratified the Constitution granted to the head of the executive branch (or any other branch, for that matter) power to prevent the people of the United States from being burdened by the cost of health care or by the pernicious practices of health care providers.

That's probably because such authority **IS NOT GRANTED IN THE CONSTITUTION TO ANYONE,** including the so-called "leader of the free world."

What should come as a surprise to no one is that many members of the president's party who called former president Barack Obama a tyrant and a wannabe king for his use of executive orders are praising President Trump for an identical usurpation.

"Patients should know exactly what their medical procedures and prescription drugs cost before they ever get a bill," said Senator Rick Scott (R-Fla.)

"I applaud the president's action to make information on out-of-pocket spending more readily available and to require hospitals to publicly disclose prices. I am fighting every day to give patients the information they need to make informed decisions for themselves and their families, and I support these efforts. Even in the hyper-partisan, dysfunctional world of Washington, D.C., creating more transparency in the healthcare system is something we must all support to help families across our nation," the Republican lawmaker added.

Partisan hypocrisy is not particularly newsworthy. If it were, there could be 24-hour news channels devoted to nothing more than running such stories without a single re-run!

What is notable, though, is when a president campaigns on a promise to eliminate a federal program — ObamaCare — and later, in an interview conducted just hours before he signed the healthcare cost transparency fiat, praises himself for saving that very program, the one he called "a disaster" while running for the office he now occupies.

In an interview broadcast on NBC, President Trump told Chuck Todd, "I could have managed ObamaCare so it would have failed or I could have managed it the way we did so it's as good as it can be. Not great, but it's as good — it's too expensive and the premiums are too high. I had a decision to make. I could have politically killed ObamaCare. I decided not to do it."

Did you see that? The president admitted that he could have kept his campaign promise and "killed ObamaCare," but he **chose** "not to do it."

Surely there will be a significant number of Republican voters who will not disregard such despotic decisions when it comes time to vote in November 2020.

The NDAA, ObamaCare, and all future and former unconstitutional acts of Congress can (and must!) be nullified by state legislators and governors. The power to negative any act of the federal government that exceeds the constitutional scope of its power is innate in the states. All observers recognize that the creature has grown so large that it threatens to consume the creator.

Chapter 13

The Right to Keep and Bear Arms

LET'S START WITH THE TEXT of the Second Amendment to the U.S. Constitution:

> A well regulated Militia, being necessary to the security of a free State, the right of the people to keep and bear Arms, shall not be infringed.

While there are admittedly an abundance of commas in that sentence, there is one period — after "infringed" — and yet Congress after Congress, Supreme Court after Supreme Court, and President after President have an obsession with treating that one period as if it were just another comma!

Given the gutting of the life-preserving liberty protected by the Second Amendment, one would think that there would be an abundance of advocates of that amendment in positions of power.

Given the role that men bearing privately owned firearms played in the history of this country, one would think there would be an abundance of academics reminding us of the details of that historical record.

Given the relatively recent role that civilian disarmament played in placing an entire people in vulnerable, defenseless subjection to tyrants, you'd think there would be an abundance of the descendants of those deceived by the despots standing as witnesses of the short road from freedom to fascism.

One would think all those things were true, but they aren't. Not one of those things is true.

Lest anyone assume that he's about to get a detailed chronicling of the confiscation of weapons throughout history, I feel compelled to remind him that this isn't a book about the history of the Second Amendment. This is a book about how states can reassert their sovereign authority to restore the full roster of liberty to the people of the united States, so while there will be historical examples used as cautionary tales, the balance of the chapter will focus on showing states how they can force the federal beast back inside its constitutional cage and thus protect their citizens' right to keep and bear arms. Period.

Let's start some recent attacks on the right to keep and bear arms.

During an interview in June 2019 with the British morning talk show Good Morning Britain, President Donald Trump told the hosts that he was going to "think about" banning sound suppressors for guns, known commonly (though incorrectly) as silencers.

Piers Morgan, an avowed advocate of civilian disarmament, began by complimenting the president for banning bump stocks, and then he transitioned to discussing the Virginia Beach tragedy, and that then led to the following exchange between Trump and Morgan.

"What is your view on silencers?" Morgan asked, after mentioning that the man accused of committing the atrocities at Virginia Beach used a suppressor.

"I don't like them," President Trump responded.

"Would you like to see those banned?" Morgan asked.

"I'd like to think about it," Trump replied. "Nobody's talked about silencers very much. They did talk about the bump stock and we had it banned. We're looking at that, I'm going to seriously look at it," the president added, referring to his unconstitutional banning of bump stocks via executive order.

This discussion was prompted by the fact that an armed man opened fire in Virginia Beach, Virginia, killing 12 people. During their investigation at the crime scene, police recovered a sound suppressor, sometimes inaccurately styled a silencer.

Now, on to the more important aspects of President Trump's consideration of making suppressors the next bump stock: a firearm accessory that he somehow believes he has the authority to outlaw by issued an executive order.

First, should President Trump's tyrannical attack on the rights protected by the Second Amendment really be surprising?

After the Parkland school shooting in the spring of 2018, during a meeting with legislators, President Trump tried to persuade them to pass a law raising the minimum age to buy a rifle and — pay attention here — regarding the use of guns to commit crime, President Trump said, "Take the guns first, go through due process second."

That's right. The president supported by the National Rifle Association (NRA) believes that police should be able to confiscate guns from Americans without a warrant, without due process, without any authority other than his own.

So-called "red flag" laws are the latest lever prying guns out of the hands of Americans.

Here's a bit of history of President Trump's "banning" of bump stocks.

Our Founding Fathers were not concerned about protecting a man's right to keep his home and family safe from "danger." Our Founding Fathers protected the individual's right to keep and bear arms because they knew that such was the only way to avoid being enslaved by tyrants.

They knew from their study of history that a tyrant's first move was always to disarm the people, and generally to claim it was for their safety, and to establish a standing army so as to convince the people that they didn't need arms to protect themselves, for the tyrant and his professional soldiers would do it for them. Sound familiar?

Consider this gem from Blackstone, a man of immense and undeniable influence on the Founders and their understanding of rights, civil and natural.

In Volume I of his *Commentaries on the Laws of England*, Blackstone declares "the natural right of resistance and self-preservation, when the sanctions of society and laws are found insufficient to restrain the violence of oppression."

Would anyone in America — or the world, for that matter — argue that the "sanctions of society and laws" are sufficient to "restrain violence" or oppression?

Thus, the people must be armed.

Commenting on Blackstone's *Commentaries*, eminent Founding Era jurist and constitutional scholar St. George Tucker put a finer point on the purpose of protecting the natural right of all people to keep and bear arms. He wrote:

This may be considered as the true palladium of liberty.... The right of self defense is the first law of nature: in most governments it has been the study of rulers to confine this right within the narrowest limits possible. Wherever standing armies are kept up, and the right of the people to keep and bear arms is, under any colour [sic] or pretext whatsoever, prohibited, liberty, if not already annihilated, is on the brink of destruction.

I doubt readers of this book need to be convinced that the men who founded our union believed that the right of the people to be armed was an essential expression of a person's God-given right to defend his life, liberty, and property.

Similarly, readers don't need to be reminded that the president is an elected federal official with very limited powers, one of which is not the making of law by signing decrees that decrease the scope of the people's liberty.

The very first line of the U.S. Constitution makes it very clear which branch of the federal government has the authority to make laws for the union: "All legislative powers herein granted shall be vested in a Congress of the United States, which shall consist of a Senate and House of Representatives."

All legislative power, not most legislating power. Also, nowhere in the Constitution is the Congress — or any other branch or officer of the federal government — granted the authority to delegate its power to another branch or officer.

In other words, President Trump is constitutionally forbidden from issuing executive orders that are treated as laws.

That hasn't stopped him or his fellow Republicans from putting the promise of "safety" above their promise to support the Constitution.

Just days after the mass shootings in El Paso, Texas, and Dayton, Ohio, left 31 people dead in August 2019, President Donald Trump reversed his earlier position and called on state and federal lawmakers to pass so-called red flag laws.

Red flag laws — also known as Extreme Risk Protection Orders (ERPO) — allow a judge to revoke a person's right to own firearms, and law enforcement to confiscate that person's firearms, if family members or other people close to that person believe him to be dangerous to himself or others and report him. As of August 5, 2019, 17 states and the District of Columbia have passed some form of "red flag" restriction on gun ownership.

In a statement issued by the White House, President Trump declared that in the wake of the horrific violence witnessed in El Paso and Dayton, he has instructed federal law-enforcement agencies to "do a better job of identifying and acting on early warning signs" of potential mass murderers, and toward that end he has ordered that the federal government in partnership with social-media companies "develop tools that can detect mass shooters before they strike."

This may strike some readers as an odd position for a president who is supported by the National Rifle Association to take, but then again, in the days after the shooting at the high school in Parkland, Florida, in 2018, the NRA also called on Congress to provide funding for states to help them pass "risk protection orders."

"This can help prevent violent behavior before it turns into a tragedy," Chris Cox, the NRA's former chief lobbyist, said in a 2018 video.

Many Republicans whose campaigns are financed by the NRA and by Americans who believe in the right to keep and bear arms as protected by the Second Amendment to the U.S. Constitution have fallen in line behind the president and are demanding that red flag laws be passed immediately.

Representative Mike Turner (R-Ohio), who represents Dayton, released a statement on August 5 advocating for the passage of federal red flag legislation. Turner wrote:

I will support legislation that prevents the sale of military style weapons to civilians, a magazine limit, and red flag legislation. The carnage these military style weapons are able to produce when available to the wrong people is intolerable.

We must pass red flag legislation to quickly identify people who are dangerous and remove their ability to harm others. Too often after mass shootings, we hear there were early warning signs that were ignored.

I believe these are necessary steps forward in protecting our country and a testament to American values, which include protecting human life.

Other prominent members of the GOP believe that the president's support for red flag laws provides political protection for them to do likewise. As reported by the *New York Times*:

Senator John Thune of South Dakota, the No. 2 Republican, told his hometown newspaper, *The Argus Leader*, that he was "confident Congress will be able to find common ground on the so-called red flag issue." Senator Lindsey Graham, Republican of South Carolina, has already proposed legislation that would offer federal grants to states to help them enact and enforce red flag laws, also known as "extreme risk protection orders."

There is nothing like a tragedy to bring out the tyrant in politicians.

Republicans in the House of Representatives are mulling an end to a recess to return to Washington to work on passing a bi-partisan red flag bill.

Writing an op-ed in *Medium*, Republican Representative Adam Kinzinger of Illinois said he's had it with "the broken record" of mass shootings followed by debates, but no substantial legislation limiting access to weapons. Kinzinger continued:

The "red flag laws" are important to preventing gun violence and I believe more states should adopt these laws that place protective orders on those with mental issues, ensuring they cannot be a harm to themselves or others. In addition to these laws, I believe it's time for universal background checks for gun purchases, raising the age to 21 to purchase a firearm, and banning certain high capacity magazines, like the 100-round drum the Dayton shooter used this weekend.

So he's another Republican who apparently honestly believes that mental illness can be solved by passing legislation to prevent access to guns. Anyone with any sense, however, recognizes that laws restricting gun ownership exist, laws against murder exist, yet we still see murders committed. Laws, by definition, will not deter those determined to break the law.

In the case of so-called red flag laws, the opportunity for abuse is immeasurable. In light of the Trump Derangement Syndrome that has affected so many since the president took office, it is not far-fetched at all to imagine a person afflicted with this mania to name Trump-supporting family members as potentially harmful and have them hauled before a judge with their rights protected by the Second Amendment in the balance.

Furthermore, as is witnessed by the increasing number of Republican lawmakers and self-described "pro-Second Amendment" advocacy groups (the NRA most notably) calling for immediate federal and state enactment of red flag laws, the political pressure to join the claque calling for such "laws" is immense, and it isn't hard to imagine a judge not wanting to make himself a martyr to the Second Amendment, particularly when such a position would make him a pariah among even those once thought to be strong supporters of the Second Amendment.

Take note of the crescendo of "conservatives" making full-throated demands that the "mentally ill" be denied the right to keep and bear arms. Each of the congressmen, senators, and state lawmakers who've joined that choir are violating the oaths they've sworn to "preserve, protect, and defend the Constitution of the United States."

And again, how motivated would Progressives be, in the current climate, to at least take a run at having pro-Trump family members and neighbors declared "mentally ill" as a way to punish them for their vote in 2016?

For those who think such a scenario is simply the rantings of a gun nut, I add these remarks made by the NRA-backed President Donald Trump, as an indication of how strongly the ant-gun winds are blowing:

> We must make sure that those judged to pose a grave risk to public safety do not have access to firearms, and that, if they do, those firearms can be taken through rapid due process. That is why I have called for red flag laws, also known as extreme risk protection orders.

As the legal process is put into motion and investigations are conducted into the circumstances of the shootings and the conditions that may have precipitated such outrages, there are important auxiliary issues to be considered, especially in light of the shameful molding of this massacre into pawns in a partisan chess match.

The forces that control or manage the jarring often violent events of the world in order to abolish liberty are neither Leftists nor Rightists, Conservatives nor Liberals, Progressives nor Tea Partiers. They are content, however, to set these antipodean axes against each other and manipulate the controversies that they might accelerate the pace of the eventual enslavement of mankind.

Of course, one of the chief aims of those so dedicated must be the eradication of the sovereignty of the several states and the liberty of their citizens, principally through the incremental alienation of the fundamental rights protected by the Constitution from encroachment of just that sort.

The right of people to defend themselves from such tyranny is an obvious obstruction lying in the path to paternalism of the would-be rulers. Therefore, the legislative annulment of the Second Amendment and the ownership of weapons as protected thereby is a priority of these embryonic masters.

In fact, the tragic violence has played right into the hand of the foes of freedom. As the blood of innocent men and women flowed, so did ink from the pens of those who would callously employ these murders for their own political ambition.

Do not misunderstand. The forces committed to severing the fetters of the Constitution are just as happy to arouse the passions of the Right as of the Left. They have no partisan preference. Their single-minded mission is to subtly shepherd this country (and all others) along the gently sloping road to Gomorrah and to accomplish this goal they will syncretize the evangelical fury of all political denominations willfully and gleefully toward the worldwide establishment of their own debauched dogma: slavery is freedom.

As with any of these federal proposals to put a comma at the end of the Second Amendment and then add any number of conditional clauses after it, there are those state lawmakers who have authored bills that would preempt any such effort by the plutocrats on the Potomac to permanently deny "dangerous" people from ever owning weapons or ammunition.

Though encouraging, these valiant efforts to void and invalidate unconstitutional acts of the federal government are few and far between and frankly, should not be so frequently necessary to prevent such pernicious and pervasive tyranny on the part of the federal government.

As it is, President Trump continues to support federal "red flag" laws and although such statutes seem unlikely to pass Congress and get sent to his desk, the fact that he would sign such a bill is a betrayal of his vow and his voters.

Let's not forget that on January 20, 2017, Donald J. Trump put his hand on the Holy Bible and swore the following oath:

I do solemnly swear (or affirm) that I will faithfully execute the office of President of the United States, and will to the best of my ability, preserve, protect and defend the Constitution of the United States.

Using the pen on his desk to issue dictatorial edicts eviscerating the Second Amendment is no way to faithfully abide by that solemn oath.

Americans committed to protecting the Second Amendment, specifically, and the Constitution, in general, are encouraged to let President Trump know that you call on him to be true to his oath office and to stop trying to shred the Second Amendment.

I'll close the chapter with logic long-forgotten, but once trusted by our Founding Fathers — the words of Cesare Beccaria on the real result of laws purportedly passed to prevent mass murders, as written in his *An Essay on Crimes and Punishments* written in 1764:

> The laws of this nature are those which forbid to wear arms, disarming those only who are not disposed to commit the crime which the laws mean to prevent.

> Can it be supposed, that those who have the courage to violate the most sacred laws of humanity, and the most important of the code, will respect the less considerable and arbitrary injunctions, the violation of which is so easy, and of so little comparative importance?

> Does not the execution of this law deprive the subject of that personal liberty, so dear to mankind and to the wise legislator; and does it not subject the innocent to all the disagreeable circumstances that should only fall on the guilty?

> It certainly makes the situation of the assaulted worse, and the assailants better, and rather encourages than prevents murder, as it requires less courage to attack armed than unarmed persons.

Chapter 14

Potomac Fever — It's Catching

I CAN'T STRESS IT too strongly: We, the People, acting in our collective political capacity as states, are the ultimate sovereigns in this Republic. The Constitution written by the delegates of the states was never intended to — and does not — grant rights, it simply protects them. And it will do so only to the degree that we, in turn, hold it inviolate and demand that its strictures be observed by those who have sworn to uphold it.

As it stands today, most people do not consider the Constitution the law of the land. In fact, they generally do not consider it all.

In fact, many of us have been trained to accept unconstitutional federal acts and executive edicts as if they were etched in stone and handed down from Capitol Hill as if it were Mt. Sinai. Many of us rightly rail against this destructive despotism, but wrongly we look to secure the support and attract the attention of seemingly sympathetic congressmen, presidents, and judges for redress. Washington D.C. is the daughter of the mother of harlots and we can't count on her to bite the hand that feeds her. We must rely on the states and the people to bust up the brothel and send the legislative ladies of the evening home to find less lascivious and criminal vocations.

Our founders would be confused by so-called "conservatives" who think the solution to the problem of growing government is an appeal to those would one way or another benefit from the expansion.

Proof of this paradox is found in the wide-eyed, never blinking stalker-like obsession of the conservative press and pundits with every word spoken and misspoken in presidential campaigns and their corresponding complete disregard for state elections.

We need to quickly realize that more often than not in our speeches and screeds we, albeit unwittingly, cede the central government powers beyond those given it by the states in the Constitution. By devoting so much attention and ink to following every gesture of the federal government and the candidates for the offices thereof we (or they, I should say) are falling for the sleight of hand perfected by the monied magicians. When we watch Washington so intently, we are following the misdirection designed to draw our attention away from the disappearance of our liberties.

Don't believe it? Test this hypothesis by asking yourself this question: Can you name a single member of your state house of representatives? Now, see how many members of Congress you can rattle off without even concentrating. If we constitutionalists spend our time, our talents, and our treasure trying to change the federal government by electing "conservative" politicians, then we are allowing the enemies of the Constitution to win the war on liberty, no matter how many electoral battles they lose.

Look, for example, at the list of donors to a senator's — even a "conservative" senator's — re-election campaign. Once seated, something wafting into the offices through the vents of the Capitol building infects the senators with Potomac Fever and they devote their time to pleasing special interest groups and PACs rather than the constituents who elected them in the first place.

Doubt it? Go to any of several websites that report campaign contributions to candidates and connect the dots. Money is the lifeblood that keeps the modern body politic alive and kicking.

In these, and in many other statements, I realize that those who slaver for the centralization of power into the hands of an elected aristocracy in Washington are using all the tools in their shed of supremacy to build a shrine to "government," an entity apart from the people that they should either detest or depend on. These pushers of the plutocracy spend treasure and talent growing the federal government, disregarding the states (with the goal of subduing them), using their mouthpieces in the state-run media to promote the falsehood that the most powerful and important lawmakers are in Washington and that the president is the "leader of the free world." The media are hired as ad men whose sole client is the federal government and the campaign is designed to create top of mind awareness of the federal government. How often are state governments, the acts and offices thereof, mentioned on television or in major news magazines and newspapers?

Occasionally, some point out, governors are mentioned, sometimes, they say, state executives even show up on this or that cable news talk show. The hosts even ask their opinion on matters of national importance. There's the constitutional rub. Think of why these governors are spotlighted. Typically, the are only given a minute or two of precious prime time when they are being promoted as an up and coming leader with "White House potential." Or, it must be admitted, when they are being tapped by the president to fill a position in his cabinet. A backhanded compliment at best, a brilliant and devious plot designed to debase states by co-opting their leaders by enticing them with the perfume of political promotion.

The alchemists of this aroma are busy introducing it to every state house and governor's mansion in America. They conjure images of a Romanesque pathway to power, a career that even a *novus homo* from "flyover country" could aspire to if he would follow his nose — right to the putrid erstwhile swamp that is Washington D.C.

There is another similarity between ancient Rome and D.C. In Rome, one of the privileges of power was a retinue of lictors who carried a bundle of rods called fasces (the source of our word fascism — no coincidence). The fasces were the symbol of the magistrate's power to exercise his will. In contemporary America, the imperial president has a cadre of faithful followers who, like the lictors that came before them, wield several sticks who gladly flog their leader's agenda and subtly subsidize his programs.

These very visible weapons of influence, intimidation, and enticement include journalists, pundits, pollsters, television anchors, and other ever-present talking heads that gladly proclaim from every available medium the magisterial message and the preeminence of the president, congress, and the courts. Twenty-four hours a day, 365 days a year, they spread the gospel of federal primacy and the urgency of all its act and decrees.

The manifold federal campaigns and elections are broadcast in brilliant color using smart boards, iPads, and virtual reality displays. One appointed expert after another analyzes every word — sometimes every syllable — spoken by candidates and they do it with cloying glee. The Left chides the Right and the Right bashes the Left with moderators doing their best to play the disinterested straight man in this pantomime of power whose plot is nothing but a series of formulaic set-ups followed by equally predictable punchlines.

What is the point of the show? The point of the show is to keep the federal government circus constantly whirling before the eyes and screaming loudly in the ears of every American, entertaining them with a show that is so simplistic as to merit constant mockery yet so sophisticated that many in the audience actually pay attention to the melodrama.

The lasting effect is that after the curtain falls (and until it raises again in a couple of years) the audience hears the words "government" or "power" and they think of Washington, D.C. It doesn't matter to the producers of the show if the audience fears, laughs, loves, or loathes the federal government so long as the recognize its supremacy and remain in awe — whether with reverence or rebellion — of its power.

This is why issues of state importance or acts of state nullification are never covered on the news channels so many of us watch. The monied cabal that fund those companies realize that any substantive mention of state government might draw attention away from Washington and that would never do.

By putting committees, caucuses, Congress, the courts, and the White House on heavy rotation the cable news outlets assist the beneficiaries of the ruse of federal supremacy in causing the people to see "the government" as something other than their own collective will. Whether they regard this organization as friend or foe, they become convinced that power resides in Washington and is either the source of succor or the citadel of corruption. Those who thrive in the shadows of the throne don't care which label citizens pin on themselves — liberal or conservative; progressive or Tea Partier — so long as "the government" they picture in their heads is located in the Capitol and not in their capital.

With all the foregoing in mind, it becomes evident that a lot of hard work remains to remove the obstacles blocking the road running from where we are to where we want to be, constitutionally speaking.

To break this fever, finally, states need to perform practically what Madison and Jefferson described on paper. They must unashamedly disregard any act of any branch of the central government exceeds the very narrow limits of its enumerated power. Any such act purporting to have the force and function of law must be considered and treated as "*ab initio*, null, void, and of no force or effect."

Only after years of consistent practice of this principle of state sovereignty and nullification will we begin to restore our republic to the four cornerstones of the of the Constitution upon which it was wisely built.

Chapter 15

Party Above Principle

AS SET OUT ABOVE, the founders created the Senate with the intent to preserve the sovereignty of the states and allow their hands to remain on the helm of the national ship of state.

In this chapter, I will discuss the primary impetus that created the 17th Amendment and allowed it to cut the cord that once bound Congress to the state legislatures.

The principal cause: party politics. The disdain of Madison for factions are so well known they don't need to be rehearsed in full. In *Federalist* 10 Madison warned that parties ("factions") would cause "instability, injustice, and confusion" in government. In fact, he argued that partisanship was the "mortal disease" that had caused the death of every popular government in history.

These parties, he explained, were "a number of citizens, whether amounting to a majority or a minority of the whole" with interests "adverse to to the rights of other citizens."

Since the days of the early republic, these parties have creeped up on the vehicle of liberty — the Constitution — and they now threaten to blow by it and leave it choking on the exhaust of partisanship.

The speed with which parties have outpaced the states' "jealousy" of their sovereignty is astounding. It has been propelled by the most unholiest of alliances: the gathering of lawmakers in Washington, D.C. and the state capitols under common national party banners.

This union of state legislators and governors with their counterparts in the national government has given rise to a foe of federalism as formidable as any that could be devised.

The "R" or "D" after a representative's name has replaced the state abbreviation in importance. The number of senators in Washington who care more for their states than for their party caucus is so small as to be statistically insignificant. Even those senators devoted to liberty and the cause of the Constitution are more often heard praising or panning a proposal from a partisan position than a constitutional one. This or that senator may rise to speak for or against a bill based on his opinion as to whether a member of his party sponsoring the bill has been faithful to the Constitution. But by including the partisan identifier in that equation, the otherwise exemplary senator serves the program of exalting party over principle.

Americans must throw their still substantial electoral strength behind candidates who eschew party labels, party promotion, and party favors in the form of money and committee assignments.

This anti-partisan obligation brings us to the final impediment — the pot of gold waiting for all the legislative leprechauns at the end of the partisan rainbow. PACs and other monied special interests will never stop dangling dollars in the face of lawmakers who depend on donations to finance the cost of campaigns. They are drawn to the seats of power because of one fact observed earlier — Congress's assumption of the right to legislate in every arena of human existence. If states commit themselves to nullifying every act exceeding constitutional authority then the central government cur will be neutered and the trough from which these PACs and lobbyists (as well as the causes and corporations whose interests they serve) will dry up and they will move on in search of a new watering hole.

The success of this solution depends on the courage, determination, and steadfastness of the American people. We must each work tirelessly to seek out and elect those men and women who cannot be corrupted by the largesse of party bosses and political action committees. We must promote candidates who will not sell their birthright of sovereignty for a mess of partisan pottage.

The potency of this remedy — the "rightful remedy" — increases or decreases in direct proportion to the amount of fight in the citizens of this country. If we continue sitting idly by as parties and PACs sell our republic to the highest bidder, while courts and congresses flout constitutional limits on their power, while presidents and congressmen create *ex nihilo* prerogatives and classes of citizens, while presidents issue tyrannical edicts demanding they be afforded the force of law, and while the widespread misinterpretation of the so-called Supremacy Clause exalts the creation above the creator.

If we continue sowing nothing of any lasting value, we will very soon reap the whirlwind while our federal republic dissolves into one consolidated national government without limit to its power or check on its exercise of it.

There are those initially predisposed to support nullification as a powerful check on the central government's tyrannical and centripetal accumulation of all powers who wonder what would be the effect of wholesale disregard of federal edicts. This question is hard to answer because, as I have shown, there have only been a few state legislatures in recent memory brave enough and sufficiently convinced of the constitutional soundness of the principle of nullification to stand up to unconstitutional acts of Congress.

Perhaps, were more citizens and state lawmakers to understand the firmness of the foundation of nullification in constitutional law and history, more of them would join the fight to free the states from the fetters of federal tyranny.

Chapter 16

WWJD — What Would Jefferson Do?

THOSE JEALOUS OF the vast powers usurped by the federal government use the mostly state-run mainstream media to brand as a "racist" or "secessionist" anyone who dares mention the concept of nullification as an answer to the growth of government or the increase in its oversight. These people, so the charges go, are wing nuts who spend time looking for commies under the bed and shooting at black helicopters. They are accused of hating government and hating the union.

To those who have been labeled a member of the vast right wing conspiracy and to their ignorant accusers I say: Read the Virginia and Kentucky Resolutions again. Nowhere in those documents do Madison and Jefferson express a desire to weaken the union or violate the Constitution. To the contrary, their express purpose is to "prevent unjust and unconstitutional assumptions of Congressional power."

As a matter of fact, Jefferson argued that if states were to secede and form a new, separate confederation, "the same difficulties might occur in the smaller union; and finally each unit fall apart into its colonial condition."

And remember, the Kentucky Resolutions were drafted by the author of the Declaration of Independence and the Virginia Resolution was written by the Father of the Constitution. These were no disloyal or seditious separatists. Their intent, their express and elegantly phrased intent, was to prevent the union they helped form from devolving into an oligarchy whose reign would be more oppressive and tyrannical than George III ever devised in his most power-addled fantasy.

When viewed under the under the clear, unbiased lens of logic, there is no way to support a claim of anti-union intent in either the Virginia and Kentucky Resolutions or in the present-day calls for nullification of the NDAA, Obamacare, firearm restrictions, or any other federal encroachment into the sovereign territory of the states.

In truth, the Constitution and the union are strengthened through the demand that the enumeration of powers listed in the first be applied in order to not fray the ties that bind them to the second. Should the general government continue pulling and pulling against the natural power of the states, then those ties will soon snap under the strain and the state will be flung centrifugally to their own devices. This prediction is no wild premonition. This scenario is the hope of statists and centralists who hope to push those who advocate for states' rights into a de facto banishment, pariahs separated economically and electorally from those of their former fellow citizens who were eager and willing to submit to the will of the (they believe) omnipotent federal government.

Then there is the Tenth Amendment.

The Tenth Amendment explicitly reserves powers to the states and the people (whether this means that some set of powers is retained by the people and were never ceded to the states is unclear and irrelevant to this analysis). The language of the Tenth Amendment would be redundant were the states surrendering by way of ratification all their sovereign powers to the general government they created.

There would be nothing left to reserve if everything was given away in the first place. Furthermore, if the states are not the parties whose contract created the general government, does the Tenth Amendment mean they are some sort of third-party beneficiary of the agreement? If this was the intent of the framers, why didn't they say so? Furthermore, if the states are the third-party beneficiaries of the constitutional contract, who are the promisor and the promisee? There is no answer because a question so asinine never occurred to the framers.

To better understand this aspect of the relationship of state to federal government, the analogy of a homeowners' association is helpful.

Often, a number of homeowners in a neighborhood will come together to improve the security, safety, and prosperity of the neighborhood by forming a homeowners association (HOA). The neighbors will draw up a covenant and grant to the HOA certain enumerated powers. Typically, the HOA will be authorized to pass rules restricting the parking of cars on the street, the length of a lawn, the color a house in the group can be painted, and how tall a home can be built, for example. Let's assume that our imaginary HOA has a covenant granting oversight of just those few areas to an HOA council. Present and future homeowners are made aware of the covenant and they are bound to conform to its mandates.

Imagine if one day, the HOA council passes a resolution mandating that every resident of the neighborhood purchase a Toyota ... a green Toyota Camry, to be precise. Inspectors hired by the HOA council are sent out to watch every house, check every garage, and verify vehicle registrations to make sure the edict is obeyed.

Would the homeowners be required to heed this resolution? Additionally, in whom would the right to decide if adoption of the car mandate was within the power of the HOA? The homeowners, of course!

Do you think the homeowners would recognize the right of the HOA council to decide the legitimacy of its car mandate? When property owners began complaining about the obvious overreach at the next general meeting of the HOA council, do you think they would be assuaged by the council's reassurance that the dictate was perfectly within its covenant authority?

What would happen if the council then insisted on the purchase and ratified its own ruling? Can you imagine a single homeowner who would accede to that sort of ordinance inanity?

Unless the states nullify each and every unconstitutional federal act, every time one is enacted, without exception and without apology, then they are no better than the homeowner in our analogy who goes out and buys a green Camry.

I can guarantee you one thing: Thomas Jefferson *never* would have bought a green Toyota Camry!

Chapter 17

"Powerful and at Hand"

ALTHOUGH IT SEEMS LIKELY that James Madison wrote *Federalist* 46 less as a handbook and more as a hyperbole, the strategy he suggests that states should pursue if they find the general government encroaching on the power they have retained to themselves, should illuminate state legislators committed to forcing the federal beast back inside its constitutional cage.

"[S]hould an unwarrantable measure of the federal government be unpopular in particular States," Madison instructs, there would be several powerful weapons in the arsenals of the states, each of which is able to destroy federal despotism and to protect the arrangement of authority created by the Constitution. Madison maintains that these mighty weapons are "powerful and at hand."

Admittedly, throughout Federalist 46 Madison insists that these weapons will never need to be wielded. They are, nonetheless, available should the — to him — unthinkable happen, that is, should the federal government "extend its power beyond the due limits."

So as not to be caught foolishly relying on Madison's promises of federal restraint, it is wise to take inventory of the arms in our arsenal, as reported by Madison.

The first of Madison's "means of opposition" to federal overreach is "the disquietude of the people." Now, were the states and the people not in such desperate need of deploying these weapons, a reader might be tempted to treat "disquietude" as a Teflon word, that is, to let the somewhat unfamiliar word slide off the surface of our understanding, seeing as how we catch by context Madison's meaning.

We are in urgent need of getting out those guns, however, so we can't let the word "disquietude" slide off our mind, we must make it stick and stick well!

Samuel Johnson's *A Dictionary of the English Language* was published in 1785, two years prior to the drafting of a new constitution at the convention in

Philadelphia and to the subsequent letters penned by *Publius* in support of the proposed constitution.

This proximity of publication justifies a reasonable reliance on the definitions written by Dr. Johnson as having been, if not particularly known to Madison, almost certainly familiar to him.

Dr. Johnson defines "disquietude" as: "Uneasiness; anxiety; disturbance; want of tranquility."

So, the transitive property of prose reveals to us that Madison predicted in *Federalist* 46 that if the federal government ever become bold enough to set its sights on usurping power from the states, the people of the states targeted by the federal tyranny would, first, become uneasy; second, get anxious about the attack on their liberty; third, they would then cause a disturbance; and fourth, this uneasy and anxious disturbance would deprive the would-be despots of their tranquility. In other words, there would be no peace until the federal authority retreated back inside the borders of its own constitutional territory.

These people would not simply sit around and shake their fists at the television as a president, a congressman, or a court repeals their God-given rights.

These people would not simply sit down and type out a cleverly worded social media post calling out the unconstitutionality of the latest federal act.

These people would not be content complaining for two or four years until the next congressional or presidential election afforded them the opportunity to "vote the bums out."

These people would not put their faith in the arm of flesh, whether it be the flesh of a political party or a preferred candidate.

These people would not be mollified by milquetoast state officials whose lips draw nigh unto nullification of the federal government's effrontery to the state's sovereignty, but whose hearts are secretly set on serving the supreme power on the Potomac so as to secure some regal recognition and reward for their obedience to their overlords.

These people would not passively put up with some small act of autocracy, satisfying themselves with their patriotic pride at living in "a republic."

These people would not fearfully plead with Washington, D.C. to protect them from the manifold menaces roaming the earth.

These people would not sing some ancient hymn praising the virtue and virility of patriots of the past, while living a life of effeminate and affluent disassociation with the courage of their forebears.

Or, to put it bluntly, these people would not act like American people.

While whipping up loud and sustained resistance to the federal government's grab for power, the people would, Madison presumed, show their "repugnance" at even a whiff of the stench of federal seizure of authority it was not granted.

Here again, the context can produce a passable appreciation of the behavior Madison was describing, but if we're serious about saving our states and rejecting every federal disregard for restrictions on its lawful domain, then we would be better equipped for that effort if we do the work of learning the prevalent or popular 18th century definition of a word. Paging Dr. Johnson!

Johnson's *Dictionary* defines "repugnance" as: "from repugnant." Scanning down a couple of lines, we come to the definition of "repugnant:" "Disobedient; not obsequious."

Disobedient doesn't need further definition, but "obsequious" might need a little deeper drilling. Obsequious is defined as: "Obedient; compliant; not resisting."

Putting together all the pieces of that puzzle reveals a picture of what Publius meant by "repugnance." Madison prophesied that should the general government over go over the wall separating its small sphere of influence from the nearly unbounded expanse of state sovereignty, the people of the states would <u>never</u> obey or comply with "unwarrantable" federal dictates. No, James Madison was certain that the people — assuming they would be of a similar stock of the people alive when he was writing the *Federalist* — would resist any and every attempt by the general government to trespass onto the sacred and set-apart land of the people's liberty.

Next in Madison's roster of resistance is "refusal to co-operate with the officers of the Union." Could any counsel be any clearer?

When the federal government makes demands on the states, the states simply refuse to assist the forces of the empire!

As I explained near the beginning of this book, Madison was certain that if the states demurred when agents of the general government insisted on their contribution to this or that act contrary to the Constitution that the feds wanted executed within the sovereign borders of the several states, then there would be little hope that the centralizers could carry out their unconstitutional programs, plans, and projects.

Every state legislature should immediately prohibit state agents and resources from being used to cooperate with the federal forces in any activity not explicitly enumerated in the U.S. Constitution as being within the territory of federal authority. This constitutionally sound strategy is known as anti-commandeering.

Put simply, anti-commandeering forbids the federal government from enjoining states to participate in any federal program that does not concern "international and interstate matters."

While this expression of federalism ("dual sovereignty," as it was named by Justice Antonin Scalia) was first set forth in the case of *New York v. United States* (1992); and was reaffirmed by the United States' highest court in the case of *Printz v. United States* (1997).

Former Arizona Sheriff Richard Mack was one of the named plaintiffs in that landmark case, and a page on the Constitutional Sheriffs and Peace Officers Association's website recounts the basic facts of the case:

> The Mack/Printz case was the case that set Sheriff Mack on a path of nationwide renown as he and Sheriff Printz sued the Clinton administration over unconstitutional gun control measures, were eventually joined by other sheriffs for a total of seven, went all the way to the Supreme Court and won.

> There is much more "ammo" in this historic and liberty-saving Supreme Court ruling. We have been trying to get state and local officials from all over the country to read and study this most amazing ruling for almost two decades. Please get a copy of it today and pass it around to your legislators, county commissioners, city councils, state reps, even governors!

> The *Printz* ruling makes it clear that the states do not and <u>should not</u> take orders from the feds. The states are constitutionally bound to accept and execute federal directives when these directives relate to matters within the metes and bounds of federal power, but in any and all matters beyond those boundaries, the feds are on their own!

Writing for the majority in the *Printz* decision, Justice Antonin Scalia explained the constitutionally correct cooperation of state and federal authority, authority created *by the states* for **their own benefit**.

> As Madison expressed it: "The local or municipal authorities form distinct and independent portions of the supremacy, no more subject, within their respective spheres, to the general authority than the general authority is subject to them, within its own sphere." The Federalist No. 39, at 245. [n.11]

> This separation of the two spheres is one of the Constitution's structural protections of liberty. "Just as the separation and independence of the coordinate branches of the Federal Government serve to prevent the

accumulation of excessive power in any one branch, a healthy balance of power between the States and the Federal Government will reduce the risk of tyranny and abuse from either front."

Without question, at least to James Madison's mind, if states follow the *Federalist* 46 formula for freedom from consolidation, we would find that the federal government would be unable to muster the men and materiel necessary to accomplishing its authoritarian agenda. Judge Andrew Napolitano expressed his belief in this thesis in 2014 while discussing then-President Obama's reticence to enforce federal drug laws in states with laws contravening them.

"The federal government does not have the person power and resources to enforce all federal laws on its own," he said. "It needs the assistance of state and local police as well. They don't have that in Washington and Colorado because marijuana is lawful there, so it might be impractical and be too costly for the feds to enforce there."

"Our home state of New Jersey could not, for example, use the police to frustrate federal law enforcement. What it could say to state and local police (is) 'you will not cooperate.' That will make federal enforcement of tighter federal gun laws nearly impossible," Napolitano added.

"If the federal government limits guns in a state, will it need the assistance of state police to enforce those limitations?" the judge asked rhetorically. "Yes, they will. And do the states have the right to refuse to enforce federal law that's against state public policy? Yes, they do. That's where we are on this."

And that's how states can use "refusal to co-operate with the officers of the Union" to stop the federal government's "long train of abuses" in its tracks.

Madison next moves on to "executive magistrates" (governors), putting part of the accountability for nixing federal attempts to annex states and make them part of the plantation on the Potomac, to subjugate state lawmakers and governors, reducing them to serfs working for the welfare of the federal lords and ladies.

Governors, Madison predicts, would show "frowns" every time the general government expected to see smiles when the state executives were presented with the details of some new program purportedly designed to "promote the welfare" of the citizens of the states.

Can you imagine such a scenario? Can you imagine there being a governor courageous and constitutionally confident in his rightful role that he would shake his head and frown at the feds, rather than nod vigorously like a poor little puppy hoping to get a treat from his master for "rolling over and playing dead" when he told him to?

Instead of the customary criticism if the federal mandate was passed by a Congress or president not of the governor's political party, or the full-throated praise of the federal program if it was the work of the governor's own party, we'd see state executives scheduling press conferences so that his colleagues in the other governor's mansions and the congressmen and the president in their marble palaces could watch them tear up a check written on the U.S. Treasury, or an executive order written on White House stationery, or a Supreme Court "ruling" looking directly into the camera and telling the federal government — any and all of the three branches — to mind their own business, then give the camera a final slow head shake and a disgusted frown.

As for state legislatures, Madison directs them to use "devices" to deny the federal government power to force its will on the people of the states and their state representatives.

Most of the ink in this book has been spilled advocating for one such device, nullification. That said, I'm not going to go further into that issue, other than to identify it as one of the "legislative devices" that should be developed by state senators and representatives for rejecting federal attempts to accumulate power.

Besides nullification, there may be more devices — in fact, there are probably as many devices as there are devisers — that could be used to cause "embarrassments" to the federal government any time it tried taking more authority than the states granted to it.

To tell the truth, it would be disappointing and, well, embarrassing if state lawmakers committed to faithful adherence to the "oath or affirmation" they made as mandated by Article VI of the U.S. Constitution couldn't come up with manifold means of making the federal government go back to its own drawing board of despotic designs.

As James Madison reckons, these "legislative devices" should not only embarrass the feds, but they should create for them and their water carriers "difficulties not to be despised."

In order to appreciate Madison's estimation of these efforts, we'll go back to Dr. Johnson's *Dictionary*.

"Embarrassment" is defined by Dr. Johnson as "Perplexity; entanglement." That makes the prospect of state legislative "devices" even more enticing!

These state-based reactions to federal overreach should catch the federal bureaucrats and legislators in a constitutional web so sound and so well-woven that the bureaucrats, congressmen, courts, agents, or presidents would weary of trying to cut the threads and unravel the knots that they would beg to be let loose and then they'd run back to the District of Columbia to come up with some other angle of attack on state sovereignty.

These webs of words, these constitutional cords, these fetters of federalism would cause the federal government "difficulties not to be despised."

Thumbing through Dr. Johnson's *Dictionary* again, we find that "difficulties" has not changed its meaning much since 1788. So, on to "despised."

The definition of "despised" hasn't evolved much either. That said, it is illustrative to read the meaning if for no other reason than to recognize the disregard and disdain that should be shown by the states to every unconstitutional act of the federal government.

Samuel Johnson defines "to despise" as "To scorn; to contemn; to slight; to disrespect."

That's right: James Madison instructs states to scorn any "warrantable" or "unwarrantable" measure of the federal government. James Madison instructs states to contemn any federal measure that would act to consolidate power into the center. James Madison instructs states to slight the agents of the autocrats. James Madison instructs states to be disrespectful to the directives that for decades have been treated as "the law" and irresistible should now be treated as "tyranny" and irrelevant.

Finally, should the states be put in the position of using Madison's "means of opposition," that opposition should serve as "very serious impediments," that is to say, they should be the legislative leg that trips the federal foot running to take over the government of the states. The "obstructions" placed in the path leading to placing states under the totalitarian rule of the federal government should, Madison insists, should be so substantial that the feds would "hardly be willing to encounter" them.

Chapter 18

"Plans of Resistance"

ALL OF THE TACTICS listed by James Madison in *Federalist* 46 that were set out in the last chapter were to be employed by the states as individual republics. When the government of a state sees its sovereignty under attack by the entity intended to be its agent — the federal government — then that state's lawmakers and governor combine to form an impregnable barrier, a barrier behind which the state's citizens may continue to enjoy, to their fullest extent, "life, liberty, and the pursuit of happiness."

Federalist 46 also sees Madison recommend responses to federal tyranny that could be made by one state in concert with others who likewise consider their constitutionally retained territory to be under attack or threat of invasion the despots in D.C.

So sanguine is Madison about the states' perpetual jealousy of their constitutionally protected sovereignty that he could not imagine any "ambitious encroachments of the federal government on the authority of the state governments [that] would not excite the opposition of a single state, or of a few states only." No, Madison genuinely perceived of a people that would be so vigilant and so virtuous that they could not look upon tyranny with even momentary toleration.

Sadly, Madison is once again found having a little too much faith in his future countrymen's love of liberty and fealty to federalism.

He anticipates that should such ambitious and unconstitutional undertakings be uncovered by the states, they would raise "signals of general alarm" that were so widely and clearly seen by other state governments that they would all come together and "espouse the common cause" of resisting the federal force.

"A correspondence would be opened," Madison predicted. His own experience in the Orange County, Virginia Committee of Safety and the critical role played by similar committees throughout the colonies undoubtedly informed his image of how future assaults by a power-grabbing central government on the liberty of the people could be defeated by communication among those fighting the common foe.

Not only would Madison wrongly assume that states would spread the word of the darkening skies that always deliver a despotic deluge, but he carried his confidence in us one step further, assuring readers of the Federalist that the states would join together and that "plans of resistance would be concerted" and that "one spirit would animate and conduct the whole."

Not so much, Mr. Madison.

States don't band together as allies battling against a common enemy whose strength threatens to subdue them all and place everything conceivable under the unchallengeable control of a central authority thousands of miles away.

No, today states joust and jostle against each other, trying to secure a spot closer to the slop being tossed out to them by the tyrant or his federal farm hands.

Every state is guilty of gluttony. With rare exception, state governors grovel at the feet of Caesar begging for concessions, hoping they'll be found in the dictator's favor, returning home with grants, contracts, or plans for federal construction in their home state that will "create jobs" or "help relieve the budget crisis" and thus assuage the public and spur them to remember the governor's "successful lobbying" when it comes time to cast a vote in the next election.

State legislators are no better. While there are a number of them that fulfill the measure of their creation by sponsoring or supporting bills nullifying unconstitutional acts of the federal government, most state lawmakers, like their companion in the executive mansion, love the largesse and recognize the realpolitik requirement that they dance to the tune played by the piper on the Potomac if they expect to attract the attention of party apparatchiks who can clear their path to political "promotion."

Undeniably, a super majority of these "representatives" of the people know that the Constitution exists, but I would bet the farm that few of them have any idea of the oath or affirmation required by Article VI of the U.S. Constitution. What's more, I doubt more than a handful would be able to tell you anything about Article VI at all, until it comes time to vote on some state measure that dares defy an existing federal "law." When that happens, everyone of those ambitious officeholders can (mis)quote chapter and verse of Article VI and its so-called "Supremacy Clause." All of a sudden nearly every one of these state legislators looking to get an audition for a spot in the congressional cast quickly remind voters — most of whom don't know better — that the Constitution "should be followed" and that the "Supremacy Clause" trumps any state desire to contradict the will of Congress.

And that, ladies and gentlemen, is how these legislative thespians show their acting chops to those making the call backs.

We'll end this section with the final front Madison identifies in his imagined resistance by the states to federal defiance of the Constitution, particularly the Tenth Amendment and the overarching principle of federalism.

"The same combinations [of states against federal encroachments on state authority], in short, would result from an apprehension of the federal, as was produced by the dread of a foreign, yoke, Madison wrote, "and unless the projected innovations should be voluntarily renounced, the same appeal to a trial of force would be made in the one case as was made in the other," he concluded.

In other words, if the states sensed that the president or Congress was confiscating the property of their people rather than protecting it; if the states saw that the federal government was forcing Americans to buy commodities or services approved by the central authority; if the states got wind of some federal plan to reduce the states to vassals of the emperor; that is to say, Madison thought it unthinkable that should Americans in the future feel the yoke of taxation, militarization, and consolidation being placed on their shoulders, they would, as did their forefathers, throw off that burden by the use of force, without regard to whether the hands trying to fix the yoke were foreign or domestic.

Sorry, Mr. Madison, but we are not our fathers' children. We are content to be keyboard warriors — pansy patriots — and to impotently shake our fists at the "federal government" so long as the wifi signal is strong, Walmart is open 24 hours, and we can buy burritos at 3 a.m. Food and games, that's all we care about. We're slouching along as ancient Romans toward the same or similar fate and we owe it all to welfare, warfare, and we-don't-care.

Chapter 19

The Dawn Of A New Day

YES, THE CLOUDS ARE black, ominous, and delivering a deluge of despotism from sea to shining sea. States are drowning and their sovereignty is being watered down. The tempest is indeed raging and Madison's "great madness" is an epidemic not only in Washington, D.C., but in state assemblies, as well.

To stem the rising tide, I turn to one of Madison and Jefferson's favorite refuges of political theory: Ancient Greece.

On the well-traveled road from Athens to Eleusis, there was a small town called Erineus. Erineus was legendary for an inn run by an infamous innkeeper. Procrustes proclaimed his unmatched hospitality. He promised a comfortable bed and protection from the elements. And, somehow, there was always a vacancy.

Weary from their journey, many travelers would take Procrustes up on his offer and unload their packs and choose a bed in the inn. Here's where the trouble started. If upon lying down in the bed the guest didn't quite fit, then Procrustes would either stretch the person or lop off his extremities until the traveler's dimensions matched those of the bed he thought would provide him rest and recuperation.

Sadly, many a fatigued fellow found out that in spite of his welcoming offer of a comfortable cot and heated coals, Procrustes was more interested in piling up the limbs of the foolish than fulfilling his promises of hospitality.

The story of Procrustes is fascinating, but what does it have to do with nullification? For years, at least since the days of the "Reagan Revolution," constitutionalists have believed the campaign speeches of candidates promising to fit themselves and their votes within the mold of limited government as formed by our Founding Fathers and expressed in the Constitution.

These erstwhile friends of the Constitution biannually draw near unto the Constitution with their lips, but their hearts, sadly, remain far from it. Too often, once the candidate becomes the congressman, he channels Procrustes and stretches or slashes the Constitution in order to make it more closely conform to (or to justify) his legislative or executive behavior. There seems to be an amnesia that afflicts elected officials once they cross the Potomac into the halls of the national government. The fidelity they swore to the Constitution is abandoned, and the Constitution is forced, like the weary pilgrim on his way to Eleusis, to endure painful tailoring according to the whims of the one who promised such comfort.

How many of the self-described "conservatives," for example, now holding office in Congress have committed themselves to tireless striving to abolish every agency, department, program, and "entitlement" that is not specifically authorized according to the enumerated powers granted Congress in the Constitution and to returning power to the states? It is easy to join in the fray and display grand gestures swatting at the gnat of "big government" while simultaneously swallowing whole the multi-humped camel that is the perpetuation of an unconstitutional bureaucracy.

Some of these new office holders have pledged to place their own political ambitions on the altar of constitutional legitimacy, however. They would, they claim, rather go home bruised and bloodied, defeated in the battle to cut the unconstitutional spending on so many unconstitutional federal programs, rather than give in and join the majority. Each of them promises to be the last man in the last foxhole. They will never compromise with those who deem certain outlays as untouchable. They will come home with the Constitution or on it, to use another ancient Greek allusion.

Historically speaking, there is very little hope that the trenches dug around congressional power will be uncovered. The tidal wave of "conservatives" that flooded Washington in the '80s (the Reagan Revolution) or the '90s (the Gingrich Revolution famous for the Contract with America) did little to permanently wash away the filth of unconstitutional spending and when the tide subsided, the silt of "same old, same old" persisted in the marbled halls of our national government and the size and scope of government continued growing.

Republicans, as well as Democrats, find ways to rationalize their support of unconstitutional legislation while claiming to support limited government, states' rights, and the Constitution.

But as all the above demonstrates so clearly, most of these lawmakers habitually betray their oaths making the act of saving our republic from ruin will be a Herculean task. It will take sincere and steadfast attention to each and every bill proposed in Congress. We must not give quarter to the compromisers and the capitulators. We must not abide the sunshine patriot and the excuses of those willing to lay their integrity at the feet of influence.

The reformation advocated for the American people weary of the biennial cycle of promises of constitutional fidelity followed within days of the discovery that many of those in whom we placed our trust are now in the cozy and familiar arms of the mistress of money and power. This misplaced trust has cost us greatly. We cannot expect to redeem our republic unless we are willing, as were our faithful forebears, to pledge "our lives, our fortunes, and our sacred honor" to the cause.

If we are honest with ourselves, using the lamp of history as our guide, we know that many of these lawmakers will betray us. They will contract Potomac Fever, which typically robs the afflicted of their memory, particularly the recollection of affirmations of affinity to restoring constitutional limitations on power. We know that there is only one potent and "rightful remedy" for this malady.

A vital distinction must be made by Americans between elected officials who improperly exercise constitutionally delegated powers and those office holders who usurp powers not within the narrow scope of the limited powers granted by the Constitution.

In the former situation, the offender(s) may (and should) be removed from office at the next election. In the latter example, however, the states as signatories to the Constitution and creators of the federal government must nullify every single unconstitutional act.

Again, as Madison said in the Virginia Resolution, "The states have the right, and are duty bound, to interpose for arresting the progress of the evil, and for maintaining within their respective limits, the authorities, rights, liberties appertaining to them."

So, what happened to that old scoundrel Procrustes? After years of successfully tricking the trusting traveler, Procrustes offered a bed to one guest too many.

Theseus, a hero famous for meting out poetic justice to the rogues of the ancient world, treated Procrustes to a bit of his own brand of hospitality. He made the deceiving innkeeper lie in his own bed, forcing Procrustes, as he had in turn forced so many others, to fit the frame or face the axe.

Likewise, we constitutionalists, we descendants of Madison and Jefferson, we watchers on the tower, we must play the role of modern-day Theseuses to the Procrustes in Congress, regardless of their enticing and convincing promises of hospitality to the Constitution. We must demand that they confine themselves and their proposals to the four corners of the Constitution, and not the other way around. We must hold them to their commitments, and if they are found to have broken their word, then we must exercise one of our available options and defend our Constitution, lest too many such cycles pass and the true form of the Constitution is left unrecognizable through the stretching of clauses and the lopping off of limits.

As the winds of statism howl and blinding debris of despotism swirls, confusing otherwise well-meaning Americans, we turn back to Madison's warning of the "gathering storm" and the "great madness" that would precipitate it. History and our own contemporary experience demonstrate that we cannot hope to simply ride out this storm. We can't rely on "conservatives" to pass this or that "good" law or repeal this or that "bad" one.

With few exceptions, our federal elected officials violate their oaths of office daily. They contribute to the cloud cover by selling their fidelity to modern-day hucksters, pushing one or another billion-dollar boondoggle. Hundreds of ambitious men and women spend millions to gain the keys to the palaces on the Potomac. Once there, they believe, they can impose their sensibilities on a less enlightened public, and maybe they'll make a dollar (or a million) and secure a lucrative, lazy lobbyist job after they've spun long enough in the right circles.

The answer to the insanity, the cure for Potomac fever, the hope of a brighter day is a found in the silver lining of state sovereignty. Not just the existence of it, but the courageous, consistent, continual assertion of it, particularly through nullification of federal acts violative of the Constitution's enumerated powers.

To use another meteorological metaphor, the illuminating rays of nullification, emanating from the potent principle of state sovereignty, can burn through the dense fog of unrepentant, unending, and unconstitutional federal usurpation.

Will there be another generation of "demi-gods," leaders with the insight, wisdom, and strength of character to derail the long train of abuses? Will the states witness the rise of a cadre of elected leaders and grassroots activists who will love the Constitution and the liberties it protects enough to resist the bribes and the siren call of Capitol Hill?

The stark and inescapable truth is that we must not be easy going at a time of such serious danger for our republic. We must be loyal where others are traitorous. We must be tirelessly engaged in the cause of defending liberty against all enemies — foreign and domestic.

We must reject the rhetoric. The biennial and quadrennial rattling of partisan sabers signify nothing. It is the hour that every man must declare whether he supports the perpetuation and protection of the Constitution of 1787 and its enumerated and limited powers or whether he supports flinging that document onto the scrap heap of history. As the Roman orator Cicero said as he spoke in the Senate against those in that body that were plotting to destroy the republic: "Let there be written upon the brow of every man how he feels about the republic."

No man can serve two masters for he will love the one and despise the other. Too many of our elected representatives wear the robes of "conservatives" while at the same time proposing and passing legislation that betrays the principles of limited power as enshrined in the Constitution. That is despicable and those people are not with us, no matter what they say, no matter which party's banner they fly, no matter what letter they put after their names.

Today is the day for the declaration of allegiances. All who care must come out courageously and proclaim their loyalty. They needn't bother drawing near us with their lips while their voting record and personal morality is far from us. We need no sunshine patriots or compassionate conservatives. We won't tolerate wolves in sheep's clothing. We will banish from the ranks of the cause of liberty all capitulators, compromisers, and cowards. We need men and women who care less for popularity or personal promotion than for the zealous defense of our country and our Constitution.

Those engaged in the fight to restore the sovereignty of states, to unapologetically nullify each and every unconstitutional act of congress, court, or president, must recall the words of Samuel Adams:

> If ye love wealth better than liberty, the tranquility of servitude better than the animating contest of freedom, go from us in peace. We ask not your counsels or arms. Crouch down and lick the hands which feed you. May your chains sit lightly upon you, and may posterity forget that you were our countrymen.

Today, consecrate yourself to the "animating contest of freedom."

Today, begin toiling in the daily reconstruction of the barriers that our Founding Fathers erected between the branches of government, between the national government and the states, and between self-government and tyranny.

Today, steadfastly and fearlessly profess your love of liberty and your devotion to principle over party.

Today, put all the enemies of the Constitution on notice: You will not retreat. Not another inch. You will not compromise. And you will not re-elect them. You will not rest until the Constitution is restored to its proper place and everyone who stands in the way is either converted to the cause or marked as a traitor.

Today, refuse to be labeled a "Republican" or "Democrat." Refuse to be pigeon-holed as a "conservative" or even a "libertarian." From this day forward, all of us — united — must proudly gather beneath the banner of the Constitution and powerfully resist being moved, mocked, or manipulated.

Finally, remember the words spoken by Edward Livingston of New York during the debates in Congress about the Alien and Sedition Act:

> Whenever our laws manifestly infringe the Constitution under which they were made, the people ought not hesitate which they should obey. If we exceed our powers, we become tyrants, and our acts have no effect.

Ask yourself three questions: Have they exceeded their powers? Have they become tyrants? Which is more seditious: to defy the Constitution or to defend it?

If we are determined, dedicated, and defiant, those who oppose the exercise of states' rights through nullification and at the first mention of such a plan race to ring the alarm bell of insurrection, may soon realize that that bell **tolls for them!**

Appendix I

Quintessence of Long Speeches Arranged as a Political Catechism (1830) (Attributed To Maria Pinckney)

Question—What do we understand by the Federal Union?

Answer—It is an agreement between Sovereign States, to forbear exerting their sovereign power over certain defined objects, and to exert jointly their sovereign power over other specified objects, through the agency of a General Government. Each State agrees to exert its full sovereign power jointly, for all external purposes; and separately, for all internal purposes, or State concerns.

Q. Where is this Agreement found?

A. In the bond of Union, or compact between the States, called the Federal Constitution.

Q. What is the nature of the Federal Constitution?

A. It is a compact based upon cautious and jealous specifications. The distinguished body of men who framed it, guarded and defined every power that was to be exercised through the agency of the General Government—and every other power not enumerated in the compact, was to be reserved and exercised by the States.

Q. Did the States, in forming the Constitution, divest themselves of any part of their Sovereignty?

A. Of not a particle. The individuality and sovereign personality of the States was not at all impaired. The States agreed, by the Constitution, that they would unite in exerting their powers, therein specified and defined, for the purpose and objects therein designated, and through the agency of the machinery therein created; but the power exercised by the functionaries of the General Government, is not inherent in them, but in the States whose agents they are. The Constitution is their Power of Attorney, to do certain acts; and contains, connected with their authority to act, their letter of instruction, as to the manner in which they shall act. They are the Servants. The power which gives validity to their acts is in their Masters—the States.

Q. Where is the power of Congress during the recess of that body?

A. It possesses no sovereign power—it is but the agent of the Sovereign States.

Q. Can you illustrate this retention of Sovereignty by the States by any other example?

A. Suppose an individual, for instance, was to stipulate to transact a portion of his business by an agent, and the remainder by himself, and to forbear to exert his moral faculties, and physical energies upon that class of subjects, which, by his agreement, are to be acted upon by his agent. Has he by his stipulation lessened, impaired, or diminished his moral or physical powers? On the contrary, the validity of the agency depends upon his retaining those faculties, for if he shall become insane, or die, the agent cannot act, because the power of his principal has become extinct; so it is the power, the full subsisting Sovereign Power of the States, which gives validity to the acts of the General Government. The validity of these acts does not result from the exercise of a portion of the Sovereign Power of each State.

Q. Why then has it been supposed by some, that when the States formed the Constitution, they cut the Sovereignty of each State into two parts, and gave much the larger portion to the General Government?

A. Many erroneous and mischievous opinions proceed from ignorance of the true meaning of words. Sovereignty, Rebellion, Nullification, &c. we hear every day used, without any precise idea being attached to their signification.

Q. What is the meaning of Sovereignty?

A. It is the will of civil society in the Social Compact, which society is a moral person, whose will, like the will of the human being, cannot be divided without destroying the person; we can conceive the will operating in a thousand various ways, but we cannot conceive its separation onto parts; neither can we conceive of the separation of Sovereignty—its unity and life are inseparable.

Q. How do you define Rebellion?

A. It is the resistance of an inferior to the lawful authority of a superior. A child may rebel against a parent—a slave against his master—citizens against the government, and colonies against the mother-country—but a State cannot rebel; because one Sovereign cannot rebel against another, for all Sovereigns are equal. The Sovereignty of the little State of Delaware is equal to that of New-York, or of Russia, though the physical power of those Sovereignties are vastly different. The supposition, therefore, that a Sovereign State can commit Rebellion, Treason, or any crime whatever, is utterly inadmissible in the science of politics. The idea of crime cannot exist where there is no conceivable or possible tribunal, before which the culprit could be arraigned and convicted. Still less can any State be supposed to incur the guilt of rebellion or treason, by resisting an unconstitutional law of the General Government. The General Government is the creature of the States—the offspring of their Sovereign Power. Is the Creator to be governed by the lawless authority of the Creature? We cannot invert the rule of reason and of law upon that subject, and say, that the superior incurs guilt by resisting the inferior, and not the inferior by resisting the superior.

Q. What is the meaning of Nullification?

A. It is the veto of a Sovereign State on an unconstitutional law of Congress.

Q. Are not unconstitutional laws, of course, null and void?

A. Undoubtedly; and an act of Usurpation is not obligatory; it is not law, and resistance is justifiable. In virtue of her Sovereignty, the State is the judge of her own rights, and bound as Sovereign to protect her citizens, which she does by nullifying the obnoxious law, and releasing them from any obligation to obey it.

Q. Has not this right of the State been denied?

A. Only by those who are enemies of State Rights, whose subterfuge is, that they can find Nullification no where in the Constitution. Suppose a State was to make a treaty with a foreign government, to coin money, to grant letters of marque, or assume any power that she had by the compact delegated to the General Government. When Congress should nullify the assumption, would the State have any right to complain that she could not find Nullification in the Constitution. If the implied right is reciprocal, the State possesses the double right to Nullify, for all rights are reserved to her, that are not specified in the Constitution.

Q. Is there no other check upon the General Government, than the one just mention of Nullification?

A. The oath, the several legislative, executive and judicial officers of the several States take to support the Federal Constitution, ought to be as effectual security against the usurpation of the General Government, as it is against the encroachments of the State Governments. For the increase of the powers by usurpation, is as clearly a violation of the Federal Constitution, as a diminution of these powers by private encroachments; and that oath obliges the officers of the several States as vigorously to oppose the one as the other.

Q. Could then any collision arise between the States and the Federal Government, were each confined to its proper sphere?

A. The Constitution has left them sufficient space to move harmoniously together; but it is the General Government that is continually wandering out of the sphere of its legitimacy, and usurping powers, that the combined wisdom of the States imagined, they had carefully guarded from all encroachments.

Q. Have the States ever resumed any of the powers they have delegated to the General Government?

A. Never, in a single instance, have they violated, or attempted the Constitution. The enemies of State Rights pretend, that had the States the right to judge of an unconstitutional law of Congress, (in other words, of an infringement on their Sovereignty) they would transcend their appropriate sphere, and usurp the powers assigned to the General Government. On the contrary, it is not the interest of the States to resume the powers they have delegated. The same motives which led to the formation of the Union, a conviction of its utility, are as strong now that its beneficial effects have been experienced, as when they were only anticipated. They have evinced from the period of its formation, no sentiment so strong, as an ardent and devoted attachment to the Union. In Union, they take their high station among the nations of the earth; and in Union, the Star Spangled Banner waves over every sea. But there is a principle we should never forget, that the greatest good when perverted becomes the greatest evil. The Union as it was formed—an Union of Free, Sovereign and Independent States—and Union, affording equal protection and mutual benefit to all, will be considered the greatest political good; but as highly as it ought to be valued, it is not the greatest possible good. There is one still better—still more precious—one which is prized infinitely higher—it is LIBERTY—that LIBERTY for which our Fathers toiled and bled. The usurpations and tyranny of Great Britain were not resisted, that the COLONIES might be FREE, and for the PEOPLE to be FREE, the STATES must be FREE. Whenever the States cease to maintain their Sovereignty unimpaired, and become vassals of the General Government. The duration of the Union will then, indeed, be problematical. It is, therefore, on the friends of the State Rights— on the supporters of State Rights—on those who cling to State Rights, as to the palladium of their liberties, that we must rely for the maintenance and perpetuity of the Union, and not on the enemies of State Rights. The weak—the timid—the apathetic, and the ambitious, who raise the cry of disunion to palsy the unity of usurpation—these are the real disunionists, and to these and these only, will be attributed, the evils arising from the dissolution of the Union.

Q. What is the new version of the Constitution by Messrs. Webster & Co.?

A. They have discovered that the Constitution was not formed by the States in their Sovereign capacity—that it is not a compact between the States—but that it is a Government formed by the people, en masse, that is, by the people collected into one nation—that this nation brought the Government into existence—

established it, and hath hitherto supported it for the very purpose, among others, of imposing certain salutary restraints on State Sovereignties. That in forming this National Government, the people conferred upon the Supreme Court, the power of imposing these certain salutary restraints upon the Sovereignty of the States.

Q. To what do these Doctrines lead?

A. To the annihilation of State Rights, and consequently, of the fundamental principles of Constitutional Liberty, for which our Fathers fought and conquered.

Q. How did they contrive to convert the people of thirteen distinct States into one people?

A. A short analysis of the process by which a State is formed, will demonstrate the impossibility. The discussion of the elements of Government is dull, as is all abstract discussion. But if we undertake to talk politics, we must undertake to know about what we talk and we cannot understand the nature of our Government, without referring to first principles.

Q. By what process are States formed?

A. There are but two conditions of mankind—the one national, and the other artificial. In a state of nature, there is no government. The laws of nature are the only rules of human conduct, and each individual is his own expounder of those laws. He is the arbiter of his own rights, and the avenger of his own wrongs. There is no power (that is, no moral power) in one man to direct, control, or govern another; all are equally free. The evils inseparable from this condition, induce those who are suffering from it to escape to the artificial state. The transition from a state of nature to that of civil society, is effected by an agreement among all who compose the society, that each and his concerns, shall be directed by the understanding, and protected by the power of all. The agreement is reciprocal. The right which each man possessed, in a state of nature, to direct himself. Is voluntarily surrendered by him to the society, and he agrees, that he and his concerns shall henceforth be subject to the will of the society. The power to govern can be obtained upon no other supposition. It is denominated the social compact. It is the charter by which civil society is incorporated, by which it acquires personality and unity; by which the action of all the people, is considered as the action of a moral agent, of a single person. This moral agent is, in reference to its own condition, called a state, probably, from the fixed and stable condition of the people, compared with their unstable and fluctuating condition in a state of nature. The people compressed or compacted with their unstable and fluctuating condition in a state of nature. The people compressed or compacted by the social compact into the unit, called a State, remains unchanged under all the changes of its Government, which accident may produce, or war or convulsion may inflict. It a Republic becomes a Monarchy, or a Monarchy a Republic, or State remains unchanged, and is Sovereign, while ever it manages its own affairs by its own will. It is upon this principle that States are not absolved from their debts by revolution. The State and not the Government is the contracting party, and nothing but the dissolution of the social compact and consequent extinction of the State, can absolve it from its payment. Much confusion has arisen from the indiscriminate use of the word State. State means the people in their political capacity, and never their government. By this reference to first principles, we find from the existing state of things—as there were thirteen distinct States at the time the Constitution was formed—that it must of necessity have been formed by the States, not by the people consolidated into one nation, for in no other way could they have been collected into one, but by first absolving themselves from their allegiance to their respective States, and dissolving the compacts by which they were formed into States. Civil Societies have been destroyed by earthquakes, by deluge, and by the exterminating ravages of war; they have often been subdued into vassalage or reduced by usurpation to the condition of the provinces, but we have no account in history of a people voluntarily dissolving the social compact. Messrs. Webster & Co's. discovery , therefore, is a proof that there is no absurdity too great for those who are determined to accomplish their views on particular subjects.

Q. Does not the Supreme Court also contend that the Constitution was formed by the people collectively?

A. The Supreme Court is the creature of the General Government, and has with a constancy and silence, like the approaches of death, adhered to a construction that has increased its own power—enlarged that of the General Government, and thrown chains over State Rights—chains never dreamed of at the formation of the Constitution.

Q. Upon what does the Supreme Court and Messrs. Webster & Co. found their discovery?

A. Upon the preamble to the Constitution—it is in these words: "We the people of the United States, to form a more perfect Union," &c.

To people of common understanding, black actually means black, and white really white; but to Messrs. Webster & Co. it means just the reverse. "We the people of the United States" means according to them—"We the people not of the United States, but the people collectively."

Q. When the States formed the Constitution, under which kind of government were they?

A. They were united by the Confederation. To form a more perfect Union of the States already united, to consolidate their Union of the States already united, to consolidate their Union, was the object of the present Constitution, and not to unite the people, for it was impossible to unite them more perfectly by a Constitution than they were already united by the social compact.

Q. What is the nature of the Supreme Court, that according to Messrs. Webster & Co. has the power of imposing salutary restraints upon State Sovereignty?

A. The epithet of supreme which gives importance to the Court and imposes on the ignorant, is entirely relative, and imports only that appellative jurisdiction which it may exercise over the subordinate Courts of the General Government. The appellative Court, or Court of Appeals of every State, is just as supreme for the same reason—it also exercises jurisdiction over the inferior Courts. It is not called supreme, in reference to the other departments of the Government, nor has it any supremacy in reference to the States. The power accorded it is purely judicial. It is the umpire in all cases of law and equity arising under the Constitution. But questions of sovereignty, policy, or expediency, are unsusceptible of its judicial cognizance and decision. That power to declare a law of Congress, or any of the States, unconstitutional, was never intended to be conferred on the Supreme Court as a direct power. The exercise of the power is merely incidental in exercising the judicial power. The Constitutionality of a law may be incidentally decided, in deciding the law and justice of a case But the decision must be given in the exercise of merely judicial, and not of political power. Can it be believed that the great men who framed the Constitution, and guarded each specification with such zealous care, ever intended to subject the whole to the control of a judicial Oligarchy? The power asserted for the Supreme Court, is superior to that of imperial Rome in her proudest days. The conquests of Rome were achieved at an incalculable expense of blood and treasure. But the Supreme Court may vassal twenty-four Sovereign States, without expending one cent or shedding one drop of blood.

If the States were but true to themselves, and faithful in the discharge of their high duties, they would move on in the majesty of their sovereign power, and maintain with a steady and equal hand both their Governments within its appropriate sphere, and not permit the mere modicum of judicial power which they have granted to the Supreme Court, to control them in the exercise of their sovereign power.

Q. Why have the States allowed the Constitution, the sacred legacy of the combined wisdom of their fathers, to be violated by sacrilegious hands?

A. Because that self interest is the governing principle of three-fourths of mankind. The North, East, and West acquiesced in the usurpation of the General Government, because it was for their exclusive benefit, while the South was passive through apathy and sleep. The North and East bribed the West by internal improvement, and by donations of the public lands—and the West in her turn, bribed the North and East with the Tariff. Internal improvement and a Tariff of protection, are twin born abominations unknown to the Constitution. The South, whose vital interests and almost her existence depended on the interests and almost her existence depended on the inviolability of the Constitution, scarcely awakened from her dream of sovereignty, finds herself the vassal province of a Consolidated Central Government, without limitation to its power, but the will of the majority to legislate for the general welfare - the very government by usurpation, that the Supreme Court and Messrs. Webster &. Co. discovered was established by the people. The usurped power is a virtual abrogation of the Constitution, and consequently leaves the minority to ruin and degradation. This minority is the South.

Q. What is the remedy for these evils, according to the submission men, [or Tories of the Revolution!]

A. To shut our eyes — hold our tongues, and fold our arms.

Q. What is the greatest anomaly at present in the Union?

A. It is, that the South, whose beau ideal was Liberty, who sacrificed to it as to the God of their idolatry, is now in vassalage to the North, East and West.

Q. To what may the patriotism of many here be likened?

A. To the philanthropists, whose charity is too exalted to relieve the misery at their own door, but are willing to bestow it on three-quarters of the globe.

Q. What is the feeling that Carolina's real sons cherish for her at this moment?

A. That feeling so touchingly and beautifully expressed by the Beaufort Orator on the last anniversary of independence. "If, in celebrations like this, the name of Carolina was unintentioned by her Orators, the omission was altogether unmarked - why was it when now you can think only of her? It was, because she had not yet been depressed into notorious inequality from the level of the majority of her Sister States. She was not yet in full possession of that deepest and most touching attractiveness, with which misfortune and the world's persecution never fail to invest a beloved object in the contemplation of the generous and brave; you had not yet felt in the cold and cutting blast of federal unkindness the necessity of cherishing and warming her in your hearts. She had been prosperous and affluent, and you but rejoiced that she was your State — she had been honoured — and you were but proud of her, as your section of the Union; but when she was injured and insulted, we felt that she was our country! And when she was most insolently trampled, we clung to her most fondly, and when they called her weakest, our hearts beat strongest in her cause."

Q. What is the attitude Carolina should assume at the present crisis?

A. She must at once appeal to her sovereignty, and decide whether she shall herself exert the protecting power of Nullification through the organs of her

Legislature, or assuming her highest attitude of sovereignty, through that of a Convention.

Q. What will be the result of this resistance on the part of the State to the obnoxious usurpation?

A. The first result will be, the preservation of her sovereignty— the next result, the General Government, no longer relying on the supineness of the State, will be driven back to the sphere of its legitimacy.

Q. But if one of these results should not folio to, must the State forbear to resist the aggression upon her rights?

A. No— decidedly no. She must maintain her sovereignty at every hazard, and every means within her power. She is good for nothing-worse than *good for nothing— without it.

Q. Will this not lead to civil war — to war between the State, and the General Government ?

A. No: The General Government would not pul itself so completely in the wrong, as to consecrate its Usurpation by the blood of those it shall have attempted to oppress. If the State is led by apprehensions of this kind to submit to oppression, there is then an end of shaking off her fetters. Fear is a bad counsellor of even an individual, it should never be consulted by a Sovereign State. The strength and powers of Usurpation consist wholly in the fear of resisting it. Let the State only will to be free, and the General Government must recede from its pretensions.

Q. But if the General Government does not recede?

A. Then let the State send a solemn embassy to the bar of Congress, and demand as a Sovereign State, one of the parties to the compact, a redress of her grievances, or an appeal to the ultimate arbiter, provided by the fifth article in the Constitution. Three-fourths of the States compose this august tribunal.* The State does not compromise her dignity, by referring to them questions of Sovereignty being-them-Three-fourths. —It has been said in a late State Paper, Hint the States by assenting to the provision of the Constitution, that three-fourths of them might amend or change it, surrendered individually their original Sovereignty, and that the Sovereignty of the Union actually now resides in three-fourths of them. This is an erroneous opinion. The States agreed that the voice of all should be expressed by three-fourths, there was no surrender of individual Sovereignty. selves Sovereign, but she cannot without violating every principle of self-respect, submit a question in relation to her sovereignty to one of her subalterns, the Supreme Court. It is in the power of this tribunal to define anew the relations between the State and the General Government; if it does not concur in admitting the contested power, or shall not pronounce that it already exists, the General Government will at once be constrained to abandon the exercise of it, for no new power could have been granted without the concurrence of this tribunal.

Q. But if three-fourths of the States, the ultimate arbiter, decide the question against the State, whose vital interest is at stake, does acquiescence become a duty?

A. The State must then calculate the value of the Union; she has always the right of secession, but we will not, even in idea, "fathom the abyss, until we have descended the precipice of disunion."

Q. On whom must Carolina depend in her hour of peril?

A. On the descendants of the patriot band who achieved the Revolution. On the descendants of those brave and generous foreigners who united with us in that arduous and glorious struggle. On the proprietors of the soil — and on those whose motto is "millions for DEFENCE, NOT A CENT FOR TRIBUTE."

Appendix II

"The Union" (From John Taylor of Caroline's *Construction Construed and Constitutions Vindicated* (1820)

Who made it? "We, the people of the United States." But who were they? The associated inhabitants of each state, or the unassociated inhabitants of all the states. This question is an exposition, either of the ignorance or the design of construction. If there is no difficulty in answering it, construction ought to be laughed at for playing the fool; but if it gives the wrong answer, as supposing it to furnish contrary inferences to the right one, it ought to be suspected of playing the knave. At least an attempt to construe away a fact, known to everybody, is a very fine specimen of its character when aiming at an accession of power. It has been imagined, that by considering the union as the act of the people, in their natural, and not in their political associated capacity, some aspect of consolidation might be shed over the country, and that the federal government might thereby acquire more power. But I cannot discern that the construction of the constitution will be affected in the smallest degree, by deducing it from either source, provided a sound authority is allowed to the source selected. Every stipulation, sentence, word and letter; and every donation, reservation, division and restriction, will be exactly the same, whichever is preferred. A man, having two titles, may distinguish himself by which he pleases, in making a contract; and whichever he uses, he remains himself. So the people having two titles or capacities, one arising from an existing association, the other from the natural right of self-government, may enter into a compact under either, but are themselves still; and their acts are equally obligatory, whichever they may select. Politicians may therefore indulge their taste in deducing the constitution of the union from either, but whichever they may fancy, no sound ground will thence result for their differing in the construction of it.

Nevertheless, to take away the pretext, however unsubstantial, for a different construction of the constitution, on account of the capacity or title under which the people acted in its establishment, it is material to ascertain the meaning of the phrase "we the people of the United States;" towards which, let us run over most of the state constitutions.

New Hampshire. "The people of this state have the sole and exclusive right of governing themselves as a free, sovereign and independent state. Every subject of this state. In the government of this state. The people inhabiting the territory formerly called the province of New Hampshire, do hereby solemnly and mutually agree with each other to form themselves into a free, sovereign and independent body politick or state. That the state may be equally represented. I do swear that I will bear faith and true allegiance to the state of New Hampshire."

Massachusetts. "The body politick is formed by voluntary association of individuals. The people of this commonwealth have the sole right of governing themselves as a free, sovereign and independent state. The people do hereby mutually agree with each other, to form themselves into a free, sovereign and independent body politick or state."

New York. "This convention, in the name and by the authority of the good people of this state. The legislature of this state. No members of this state shall be disfranchised. Delegates to represent this state in the general congress of the United States. Be it enacted by the people of the state."

Pennsylvania. "We the people of the commonwealth of Pennsylvania ordain. The legislature of a free state. All government originates from the people and is founded in compact only."

Delaware. "The people of this state. The government shall be called the Delaware state. The legislature of this state. The general assembly of this state. There shall be no establishment of any one religious sect in this state."

Maryland. "The people of this state ought to have the sole and exclusive right of regulating the internal government thereof. The legislature of this state. The delegates to congress from this state shall be chosen by joint ballot of both houses of assembly. I will be faithful and bear true allegiance to the state."

Virginia. "All power is derived from the people. Magistrates are their trustees or servants. A well regulated militia is the proper defence of a free state."

North Carolina. "The people of this state have the sole and exclusive right of regulating the internal government thereof. Monopolies are contrary to the genius of a free state. All commissions shall run in the name of the state of North Carolina. The legislature of this state. The constitution of this state."

South Carolina. "The legislative authority of this state. The several election districts in this state shall elect. The style of process shall be "The state of South Carolina, and conclude against the peace and dignity of the state." I swear to preserve the constitution of this state and of the United States."

Georgia. "Members of the legislature shall swear to promote the good of the state, to bear true allegiance to the same, and to observe the constitution. To make laws necessary for the good of the state. Citizens and inhabitants of this state."

Vermont. "The people are the sole source of power. They have the exclusive right of internal government. All officers of government are their servants. Legislative and executive business of this state. The people have a right to exact from their legislators and magistrates the good government of the state. The legislature of a free and sovereign state. Shall be entitled to all the privileges of a freeman of this state. Every officer shall swear to be faithful to the state of Vermont, and to do nothing injurious to the constitution or government thereof."

Without further quotations, let us demonstrate the force of these, extracted from a majority of the state constitutions, to fix the meaning of the term "state" according to the publick judgment, by substituting the word "government" for it. They would then read as follows."

"The people of this government have the sole and exclusive right of governing themselves as a free, sovereign and independent government."

"In the government of this government."

"That the government may be equally represented."

"The people of this government ought to have the sole and exclusive right of regulating the internal government thereof."

"The legislature of this government."

"I will be faithful and bear true allegiance to the government."

"The several election districts in this government shall elect."

"Members of the legislature shall swear to promote the good of the government and to make laws for the good of the government."

"Citizens and inhabitants of this government."

"The people have a right to exact from their legislators and magistrates the good government of the government."

"Commissions shall be in the name of the freemen of the government."

It would be an incivility to the reader, to subjoin to these quotations, many arguments, to prove, that the term "state" is not in any one instance used in reference to all the people of the United States, either as composing a single state, or as being about to compose a single state. Used geographically, it refers to state territory; used politically, it refers to the inhabitants of this territory, united by mutual consent into a civil society. The sovereignty of this association, the allegiance due to it, and its right to internal government, are all positively asserted. The terms "state and government" far from being synonimous [sic], are used to convey different ideas; and the latter is never recognised as possessing any species of sovereignty.

It next behooves us to consider whether the term "states" has changed its meaning, by being transplanted from its original nursery, into the constitution of the United States; and is there used to designate all the inhabitants of the United States, as constituting one great state; or whether it is recognised in the same sense in which it had been previously used by most or all of the state constitutions.

The plural "states" rejects the idea that the people of all the states considered themselves as one state. The word "united" is an averment of pre-existing social compacts, called states; and these consisted of the people of each separate state. It admits the existence of political societies able to contract with each other, and who had previously contracted. And the words "more perfect union" far from implying that the old parties to the old union were superseded by new parties, evidently mean that these same old parties were about to amend their old union.

But the parties, though recognised as being the same, were not strictly so. The authority of the people of each state is resorted to in the last union, in preference to that of the government of each state, by which the old confederation was formed. This circumstance by no means weakens the force of the last observation, because the recognition of existing political parties able to contract, remains the same.

The states, in referring to the old union, only admit themselves to have been bound by their governments, as they possessed the right of making treaties. But as the state governments were the parties to the first confederation, and as such, had a mutual right to destroy that treaty, this danger suggests another reason for the style and principles of the new union. Among its improvements, that by which it is chiefly made "more perfect," was the substitution of the authority of "the people of the United States" for that of the governments of the United States; not with an intention of excluding from the new union the idea of a compact between the states, but of placing that compact upon better ground, than that upon which it previously rested.

The term "union" has never been applied to describe a government, established by the consent of individuals; nor do any of our state constitutions use it in that sense. They speak indeed of individuals "uniting" to form a government, not to form a union; and I do not recollect that a single compact between individuals for the establishment of a government, has ever been called a union; though a multitude of cases exist, in which that name has been given to agreements between independent states. If therefore this term comprised the whole evidence, to prove that our union was the act of distinct bodies politick, composed of the people within different geographical boundaries, and not of a number of people, encircled by one line, without any such discrimination, it would be sufficient.

But the constitution itself furnishes the plainest correspondent evidence, in its origin, establishment and terms. The members of the convention which formed it, were chosen by states, and voted by states, without any regard to the number of people in each state. It was adopted by thirteen votes, without respecting the same principle. Now what was represented by these voters; the territory of each state, or the people of each state? The terms "United States" must refer to one or the other. If to the former, then the territories of each state entered into a compact "to form a more perfect union, establish justice, insure domestick [*sic*] tranquillity, provide for the common defence, promote the general welfare, and secure the blessings of liberty to ourselves and our posterity." The posterity of territories. If to the latter, it was the people of each state, who by compact in their political capacity, by giving one vote each, formed the union.

The concords with this opinion present themselves at every step, throughout the compact.

The house of representatives are to be chosen by the people of the several states, not by the people comprised within the territories of all. The right of choice is confined to the electors of the most numerous branch of the state legislatures. Thus the right of suffrage is placed upon different grounds in different states. Had the constitution of the United States been the act of all the people inhabiting the territory of the United States, this right would have been made uniform; but being the act of the people of each state, in their existing political capacity, the right of suffrage of course remained as it had been settled by each in forming its society.

Each state may elect these representatives by a general ticket, as some have done; and however they may have districted themselves by their own act for their own reasons, the recognizance of state individuality by the constitution is as strong, as if they had not done so. The modes of choosing both the president and senate, coincide also with the opinion, that the constitution considered the union as the act of bodies politick called states; and not as the act of a consolidated nature; and it seems to have settled its own construction, by providing in the case of no election of a president by electors, that he shall be chosen by the house of representatives, "the votes to be taken by states, the representation from each state having one vote."

As the great political departments of the federal government, legislative and executive, emanated from the societies called states, so they are made dependent upon them, in the mode prescribed for amending the constitution of the union; because the authors had the right of altering their own work. Had this constitution originated from, or been made by the people inhabiting the territories of the whole union, its amendment would have remained to them, as the amendment of the state constitutions belongs to the people of a state. But as such a body of associated people, did not exist, the amendment of the union is left in the hands of the existing bodies politick, to which, as its authors, it obviously belonged. No majority in congress can either call a convention, or amend the constitution; but the legislatures of two-thirds of the states may compel congress to call one, and those of three-fourths, may amend it. Thus a supremacy of the states, not only over congress, but over the whole constitution, is twice acknowledged; first, by their power over the legislative and executive departments instituted for executing the union; and secondly, by their power over the union itself. I cannot conceive that the constitution could have contained any thing more hostile to the doctrine "that the sovereignty or supremacy over the government of the union, rested in the people of the United States, not in their political, but natural capacity." It clearly discloses an opinion, that there were no such people, politically speaking; nor can I discern a vestige of the people inhabiting the territories of the United States, having ever formed themselves, or attempted to form themselves, into any political society or civil government. By this new doctrine, however, the checks provided to control the powers of the government of the union are ingeniously evaded. It asserts, that the government of the union is responsible to the sovereignty of the people residing throughout the union, and not to the sovereignty of the people residing in each state. Now as an effective sovereignty of the people can only result from their having constituted themselves into a civil society, and the first people having never done so, an acknowledgment of a sovereignty which does not exist, only annuls that which does; and escapes altogether from any species of loyalty to this superior authority. It brings us back to the old ground of a tacit compact between governments and subjects. The people of each state invested their governments with limited powers. They have also established a government of the union with powers infinitely more limited, than those originally bestowed on the state governments. But if a tacit social compact between this last government, and the people individually of all the states, should be admitted, all these specifications would be abolished; because, as it is unwritten, the government of the union might construe it as was most convenient to itself, as all governments have done, which have condescended to acknowledge implied obligations only. The only difference between the Europeans and ourselves would be, that though some of their governments hardly allow of this silent social compact, none acknowledge the sovereignty of the people; whereas here this sovereignty would be denied, where it operatively exists, and acknowledged, where it does not exist at all; so that we should still possess over the government of the union, all the advantages generally reaped from "we are, gentlemen, your most obedient servants," whilst the story of Saturn would be gradually reversed.

The eleventh amendment prohibits a construction by which the rights retained by the people shall be denied or disparaged; and the twelfth "reserves to the states respectively or to the people the powers not delegated to the United States, nor prohibited to the states." The precision of these expressions is happily contrived to defeat a construction, by which the origin of the union, or the sovereignty of the states, could be rendered at all doubtful. "Powers are reserved to the people." "The people," says Johnson, are "those who compose a community." In a political instrument, the term exclusively possesses a collective, inclusive, and social sense, and is never used to describe a number of men in a state of nature. A people is a collective being. No people or community has ever been composed in the United States, except by the inhabitants of each state, associating distinctly from every other state, by their own separate consent. Thus a people in each state was constituted, and these separate communities confederated, first by the instrumentality of their separate governments, and secondly by the separate authority of the people composing each state. Common consent is necessary to constitute a people, and no such consent, expressly or impliedly, can be shown, by which all the inhabitants of the United States have ever constituted themselves into one people. This could not have been effected without destroying every people constituted within each state, as one political being called a people cannot exist within another.

The rights of a people are indivisible; and if a great people be compounded of several smaller nations, as it inherently possesses the right of self-government, it must absorb the same right of self-government in its component parts; just as the rights of individuals are absorbed by the communities into which they constitute themselves. Therefore had a people been constituted, by melting down the little nations into one great nation, those little nations must have lost the right of self-government, because they would no longer have been a people. As it was never imagined, that the individuals inhabiting all the states had constituted themselves into one people, so there has never appeared from this imaginary body politick, the least attempt towards claiming or exercising the right of self-government; nor is the government of the union subjected to its controul [*sic*] or modification. Not a single one of the United States would have consented to have dissolved its people, to have reunited them into one great people, and to have received state governments or unrestricted legislation from this great people, so ignorant of local circumstances, and so different in local habits. This reasoning would I think have been sufficient to ascertain the people by whom the constitution was made, had it contained no internal evidence of the sense in which it uses that term. But if the phrase "we the people of the United States" refers to the people of each state, the argument is superfluous, and the decision of the constitution itself, decisive.

The powers reserved are those "not delegated by the constitution." They could only be reserved by those who possessed them. They were not powers possessed by a consolidated people of all the states, but by a distinct people of each state; and as those who reserved were those who delegated, it follows, either that the reservation was to a consolidated people of all the states, or that the delegation of powers flowed from the people of the separate states. Perhaps the interpolation of a grantor and reserver of powers into the constitution, who had nothing either to grant or to reserve, may have arisen from an erroneous construction of the word "or." If the remark just made is correct, consistency decides its true meaning. "Are reserved to the states respectively or to the people." This word is used either to couple synonyms, or to denote opposition. The words "states and people" had the same, and also a different meaning: The same, as an associated people constituted a state; and a different meaning, from the right of self-government attached to mankind. But another construction seems to me to be the true one. "Or" is used merely to conjoin two words considered as completely synonymous; and the latter is introduced as an expletive of the former, lest it should be interpreted to mean "governments." The word "states" had been so often used in the constitution, that it was necessary to fix its meaning; and this amendment was intended to remove the suspicion of a tendency in the constitution towards consolidation, with which it had been charged previously to its adoption; by defining "states and people" as words synonymously used, effectually to defeat the pretense, that the term "people" meant the people of all the states, instead of the people, "respectively" of each state. A construction which supposes that all the inhabitants of all the states, and not the people of each state, were meant, would produce consequences which never could have been contemplated. The reservation would have been in favour of two incongruous objects, and therefore both could not reap its benefits. Being in the disjunctive, it might have been fulfilled by acknowledging the right of either, although the other should get nothing. By selecting the inhabitants of all the states in one mass, as the assignee of the reserved powers, the government of the union might extend their own powers; since there could be no loss, in conceding powers to those who could neither receive, exercise, nor preserve them.

In one other view, highly gratifying, these two amendments correspond with the construction I contend for. Several previous amendments had stipulated for personal or individual rights, as the government of the union was invested with a limited power of acting upon persons; these stipulate for political conventional rights. But different modes are pursued. By the first, certain specified aggressions are forbidden; by the second, all the rights and powers not delegated are reserved. The first mode is imperfect, as the specified aggressions may be avoided, and yet oppression might be practised in other forms. By the second, specification is transferred to the government of the union; and the states, instead of being the grantees of limited rights, which might have been an acknowledgment of subordination, are the grantors of limited powers; and retain a supremacy which might otherwise have been tacitly conceded, as has been often done by the acceptance of franchises from monarchs or other sovereigns. Thus the powers reserved are only exposed to specified deductions, whilst those delegated are limited, with an injunction that the enumeration of certain rights shall not be construed to disparage those retained though not specified, by not having been parted with. The states, instead of receiving, bestowed powers; and in confirmation of their authority, reserved every right they had not conceded, whether it is particularly enumerated, or tacitly retained. Among the former, are certain modes by which they can amend the constitution; among the latter, is the original right by which they created it.

When we have discovered who made a treaty, we have also discovered where the right of construction resides. Mr. Jefferson, Mr. Pinkney, Mr. Marshall, and Mr. Gerry, in their negotiations with revolutionary France, have furnished us with an admirable treatise, both to fix the residence of the right, and to display the wantonness of construction, assumed without right. Presidents Washington and Adams, all the successive members of the cabinet and congress itself, concurred in the principles advanced by these gentlemen. They prove, that an exclusive right of construction in one party, is a degradation of the other to a state of inferiority and dependance. Their arguments might be applied with great force in many views to our subject. If the states made the union, they demonstrate, that the same consent, necessary to create, is necessary to construe. Where-ever the creating consent resided, there we are directed to look for the construing consent. It would be a much grosser violation of their principles, for no party to a treaty to usurp an exclusive right of construing it, than for one party to do so. As neither the executive, legislative nor judicial departments of the state or federal governments have ever consented to the union, no one of these departments can have an exclusive right of construing it. But if they did consent, and by that consent are parties, still the right is mutual. And if they are all to be considered as the co-ordinate departments or creatures of "the people of the United States," they derive a mutual right of construction, from the mutual right possessed by the states which they represent. Suppose our legislative and judicial departments had fixed their own rights by a treaty between themselves, in the words of the general or state constitutions; would not each have possessed an unsubservient right of construction? If this right would be mutual in the case supposed, what hinders it from being also mutual, if these departments are created by an authority superior to both, and invested with distinct and limited agencies. Each trustee is subject to the supervision of his employer, and neither liable to a usurpation of another, any more than several co-ordinate ambassadors, would be to a claim of one to prescribe the duties of the rest, and regulate their consciences. It is easiest for an exclusive power of construction, where the limits of respective territories are hardest to define, to make conquests which will destroy balances, and break down restrictions; and therefore its interdiction in such cases is more necessary, than in others.

I conclude this section with a quotation from the *Federalist*. "The assent and ratification of the people, not as individuals composing one entire nation, but as composing the distinct and independent states to which they belong, are the sources of the constitution. It is therefore not a national, but a federal compact."

Appendix III

Letter of The President of the Federal Convention, Dated September 17, 1787, to the President of Congress, Transmitting the Constitution

In Convention, September 17, 1787

Sir,

We have now the honor to submit to the consideration of the United States in Congress assembled, that Constitution which has appeared to us the most advisable.

The friends of our country have long seen and desired, that the power of making war, peace, and treaties, that of levying money and regulating commerce, and the correspondent executive and judicial authorities should be fully and effectually vested in the general government of the Union: But the impropriety of delegating such extensive trust to one body of men is evident-Hence results the necessity of a different organization.

It is obviously impracticable in the federal government of these states, to secure all rights of independent sovereignty to each, and yet provide for the interest and safety of all: Individuals entering into society, must give up a share of liberty to preserve the rest. The magnitude of the sacrifice must depend as well on situation and circumstance, as on the object to be obtained. It is at all times difficult to draw with precision the line between those rights which must be surrendered, and those which may be reserved; and on the present occasion this difficulty was increased by a difference among the several states as to their situation, extent, habits, and particular interests.

In all our deliberations on this subject we kept steadily in our view, that which appears to us the greatest interest of every true American, the consolidation of our Union, in which is involved our prosperity, felicity, safety, perhaps our national existence. This important consideration, seriously and deeply impressed on our minds, led each state in the Convention to be less rigid on points of inferior magnitude, than might have been otherwise expected; and thus the Constitution, which we now present, is the result of a spirit of amity, and of that mutual deference and concession which the peculiarity of our political situation rendered indispensable.

That it will meet the full and entire approbation of every state is not perhaps to be expected; but each will doubtless consider, that had her interest been alone consulted, the consequences might have been particularly disagreeable or injurious to others; that it is liable to as few exceptions as could reasonably have been expected, we hope and believe; that it may promote the lasting welfare of that country so dear to us all, and secure her freedom and happiness, is our most ardent wish.

With great respect, We have the honor to be, Sir,
Your Excellency's most obedient and humble servants,

GEORGE WASHINGTON, President.
By unanimous Order of the Convention.
His Excellency the PRESIDENT of CONGRESS.

Appendix IV

Resolution of Congress of September 28, 1787, Submitting the Constitution to the Several States

Friday Sept. 28. 1787

Congress assembled present New Hampshire Massachusetts Connecticut New York New Jersey Pennsylvania. Delaware Virginia North Carolina South Carolina and Georgia and from Maryland Mr Ross

Congress having received the report of the Convention lately assembled in Philadelphia

Resolved Unanimously that the said Report with the resolutions and letter accompanying the same be transmitted to the several legislatures in Order to be submitted to a convention of Delegates chosen in each state by the people thereof in conformity to the resolves of the Convention made and provided in that case.

Appendix V

Madison's "Report on The Virginia Resolutions" (1800)

Report of the Committee to whom were referred the Communications of various State, relative to the Resolutions of the last General Assembly of this State, concerning the Alien and Sedition Laws.

Whatever room might be found in the proceedings of some of the states, who have disapproved of the resolutions of the General Assembly of this commonwealth, passed on the 21st day of December, 1798, for painful remarks on the spirit and manner of those proceedings, it appears to the committee most consistent with the duty, as well as dignity, of the General Assembly, to hasten an oblivion of every circumstance which might be construed into a diminution of mutual respect, confidence, and affection, among the members of the Union.

The committee have deemed it a more useful task to revise, with a critical eye, the resolutions which have met with their disapprobation; to examine fully the several objections and arguments which have appeared against them; and to inquire whether there can be any errors of fact, of principle, or of reasoning, which the candor of the General Assembly ought to acknowledge and correct.

The first of the resolutions is in the words following:—

"Resolved, That the General Assembly of Virginia doth unequivocally express a firm resolution to maintain and defend the Constitution of the United States, and the Constitution of this state, against every aggression, either foreign or domestic; and that they will support the government of the United States in all measures warranted by the former."

No unfavorable comment can have been made on the sentiments here expressed. To maintain and defend the Constitution of the United States, and of their own state, against every aggression, both foreign and domestic, and to support the government of the United States in all measures warranted by their Constitution, are duties which the General Assembly ought always to feel, and to which, on such an occasion, it was evidently proper to express their sincere and firm adherence.

In their next resolution—

"The General Assembly most solemnly declares a warm attachment to the union of the states, to maintain which it pledges all its powers; and that, for this end, it is their duty to watch over and oppose every infraction of those principles which constitute the only basis of that Union, because a faithful observance of them can alone secure its existence and the public happiness."

The observation just made is equally applicable to this solemn declaration of warm attachment to the Union, and this solemn pledge to maintain it; nor can any question arise among enlightened friends of the Union, as to the duty of watching over and opposing every infraction of those principles which constitute its basis, and a faithful observance of which can alone secure its existence, and the public happiness thereon depending.

The third resolution is in the words following:—

"That this Assembly doth explicitly and peremptorily declare, that it views the powers of the federal government, as resulting from the compact to which the states are parties, as limited by the plain sense and intention of the instrument constituting that compact—as no further valid than they are authorized by the grants enumerated in that compact; and that, in case of a deliberate, palpable, and dangerous exercise of other powers, not granted by the said compact, the states who are parties thereto have the right, and are in duty bound, to interpose, for arresting the progress of the evil and for maintaining, within their respective limits, the authorities, rights, and liberties, appertaining to them."

On this resolution the committee have bestowed all the attention which its importance merits. They have scanned it not merely with a strict, but with a severe eye; and they feel confidence in pronouncing that, in its just and fair construction, it is unexceptionably true in its several positions, as well as constitutional and conclusive in its inferences.

The resolution declares, first, that "it views the powers of the federal government as resulting from the compact to which the states are parties;" in other words, that the federal powers are derived from the Constitution; and that the Constitution is a compact to which the states are parties.

Clear as the position must seem, that the federal powers are derived from the Constitution, and from that alone, the committee are not unapprized [sic] of a late doctrine which opens another source of federal powers, not less extensive and important than it is new and unexpected. The examination of this doctrine will be most conveniently connected with a review of a succeeding resolution. The committee satisfy themselves here with briefly remarking that, in all the contemporary discussions and comments which the Constitution underwent, it was constantly justified and recommended on the ground that the powers not given to the government were withheld from it; and that, if any doubt could have existed on this subject, under the original text of the Constitution, it is removed, as far as words could remove it, by the 12th amendment, now a part of the Constitution, which expressly declares, "that the powers not delegated to the United States by the Constitution, nor prohibited by it to the states, are reserved to the states respectively, or to the people."

The other position involved in this branch of the resolution, namely, "that the states are parties to the Constitution," or compact, is, in the judgment of the committee, equally free from objection. It is indeed true that the term "states" is sometimes used in a vague sense, and sometimes in different senses, according to the subject to which it is applied. Thus it sometimes means the separate sections of territory occupied by the political societies within each; sometimes the particular governments established by those societies; sometimes those societies as organized into those particular governments; and lastly, it means the people composing those political societies, in their highest sovereign capacity. Although it might be wished that the perfection of language admitted less diversity in the signification of the same words, yet little inconvenience is produced by it, where the true sense can be collected with certainty from the different applications. In the present instance, whatever different construction of the term "states," in the resolution, may have been entertained, all will at least concur in that last mentioned; because in that sense the Constitution was submitted to the "states;" in that sense the "states" ratified it; and in that sense of the term "states," they are consequently parties to the compact from which the powers of the federal government result.

The next position is, that the General Assembly views the powers of the federal government "as limited by the plain sense and intention of the instrument constituting that compact," and "as no further valid than they are authorized by the grants therein enumerated." It does not seem possible that any just objection can lie against either of these clauses. The first amounts merely to a declaration that the compact ought to have the interpretation plainly intended by the parties to it; the other, to a declaration that it ought to have the execution and effect intended by them. If the powers granted be valid, it is solely because they are granted; and if the granted powers are valid because granted, all other powers not granted must not be valid.

The resolution, having taken this view of the federal compact, proceeds to infer, "That, in case of a deliberate, palpable, and dangerous exercise of other powers, not granted by the said compact, the states, who are parties thereto, have the right, and are in duty bound, to interpose for arresting the progress of the evil, and for maintaining, within their respective limits, the authorities, rights, and liberties, appertaining to them."

It appears to your committee to be a plain principle, founded in common sense, illustrated by common practice, and essential to the nature of compacts, that, where resort can be had to no tribunal superior to the authority of the parties, the parties themselves must be the rightful judges, in the last resort, whether the bargain made has been pursued or violated. The Constitution of the United States was formed by the sanction of the states, given by each in its sovereign capacity. It adds to the stability and dignity, as well as to the authority, of the Constitution, that it rests on this legitimate and solid foundation. The states, then, being the parties to the constitutional compact, and in their sovereign capacity, it follows of necessity that there can be no tribunal, above their authority, to decide, in the last resort, whether the compact made by them be violated; and consequently, that, as the parties to it, they must themselves decide, in the last resort, such questions as may be of sufficient magnitude to require their interposition.

It does not follow, however, because the states, as sovereign parties to their constitutional compact, must ultimately decide whether it has been violated, that such a decision ought to be interposed either in a hasty manner or on doubtful and inferior occasions. Even in the case of ordinary conventions between different nations, where, by the strict rule of interpretation, a breach of a part may be deemed a breach of the whole,—every part being deemed a condition of every other part, and of the whole,—it is always laid down that the breach must be both willful and material, to justify an application of the rule. But in the case of an intimate and constitutional union, like that of the United States, it is evident that the interposition of the parties, in their sovereign capacity, can be called for by occasions only deeply and essentially affecting the vital principles of their political system.

The resolution has, accordingly guarded against any misapprehension of its object, by expressly requiring, for such an interposition, "the case of a deliberate, palpable, and dangerous breach of the Constitution, by the exercise of powers not granted by it." It must be a case not of a light and transient nature, but of a nature dangerous to the great purposes for which the Constitution was established. It must be a case, moreover, not obscure or doubtful in its construction, but plain and palpable. Lastly, it must be a case not resulting from a partial consideration or hasty determination, but a case stamped with a final consideration and deliberate adherence. It is not necessary, because the resolution does not require, that the question should be discussed, how far the exercise of any particular power, ungranted by the Constitution, would justify the interposition of the parties to it. As cases might easily be stated, which none would contend ought to fall within that description,—cases, on the other hand, might, with equal ease, be stated, so flagrant and so fatal as to unite every opinion in placing them within the description.

But the resolution has done more than guard against misconstruction, by expressly referring to cases of a deliberate, palpable, and dangerous nature. It specifies the object of the interposition, which it contemplates to be solely that of arresting the progress of the evil of usurpation, and of maintaining the authorities, rights, and liberties, appertaining to the states as parties to the Constitution.

From this view of the resolution, it would seem inconceivable that it can incur any just disapprobation from those who, laying aside all momentary impressions, and recollecting the genuine source and object of the Federal Constitution, shall candidly and accurately interpret the meaning of the General Assembly. If the deliberate exercise of dangerous powers, palpably withheld by the Constitution, could not justify the parties to it in interposing even so far as to arrest the progress of the evil, and thereby to preserve the Constitution itself, as well as to provide for the safety of the parties to it, there would be an end to all relief from usurped power, and a direct subversion of the rights specified or recognized under all the state constitutions, as well as a plain denial of the fundamental principle on which our independence itself was declared.

But it is objected, that the judicial authority is to be regarded as the sole expositor of the Constitution in the last resort; and it may be asked for what reason the declaration by the General Assembly, supposing it to be theoretically true, could be required at the present day, and in so solemn a manner.

On this objection it might be observed, first, that there may be instances of usurped power, which the forms of the Constitution would never draw within the control of the judicial department; secondly, that, if the decision of the judiciary be raised above the authority of the sovereign parties to the Constitution, the decisions of the other departments, not carried by the forms of the Constitution before the judiciary, must be equally authoritative and final with the decisions of that department. But the proper answer to the objection is, that the resolution of the General Assembly relates to those great and extraordinary cases, in which all the forms of the Constitution may prove ineffectual against infractions dangerous to the essential rights of the parties to it. The resolution supposes that dangerous powers, not delegated, may not only be usurped and executed by the other departments, but that the judicial department, also, may exercise or sanction dangerous powers beyond the grant of the Constitution; and, consequently, that the ultimate right of the parties to the Constitution, to judge whether the compact has been dangerously violated, must extend to violations by one delegated authority as well as by another—by the judiciary as well as by the executive, or the legislature.

However true, therefore, it may be, that the judicial department is, in all questions submitted to it by the forms of the Constitution, to decide in the last resort, this resort must necessarily be deemed the last in relation to the authorities of the other departments of the government; not in relation to the rights of the parties to the constitutional compact, from which the judicial, as well as the other departments, hold their delegated trusts. On any other hypothesis, the delegation of judicial power would annul the authority delegating it; and the concurrence of this department with the others in usurped powers, might subvert forever, and beyond the possible reach of any rightful remedy, the very Constitution which all were instituted to preserve.

The truth declared in the resolution being established, the expediency of making the declaration at the present day may safely be left to the temperate consideration and candid judgment of the American public. It will be remembered, that a frequent recurrence to fundamental principles is solemnly enjoined by most of the state constitutions, and particularly by our own, as a necessary safeguard against the danger of degeneracy, to which republics are liable, as well as other governments, though in a less degree than others. And a fair comparison of the political doctrines not unfrequent [sic] at the present day, with those which characterized the epoch of our revolution, and which form the basis of our republican constitutions, will best determine whether the declaratory recurrence here made to those principles ought to be viewed as unseasonable and improper, or as a vigilant discharge of an important duty. The authority of constitutions over governments, and of the sovereignty of the people over constitutions, are truths which are at all times necessary to be kept in mind; and at no time, perhaps, more necessary than at present.

These observations appear to form a satisfactory reply to every objection which is not founded on a misconception of the terms employed in the resolutions. There is one other, however, which may be of too much importance not to be added. It cannot be forgotten that, among the arguments addressed to those who apprehended danger to liberty from the establishment of the general government over so great a country, the appeal was emphatically made to the intermediate existence of the state governments between the people and that government, to the vigilance with which they would descry the first symptoms of usurpation, and to the promptitude with which they would sound the alarm to the public. This argument was probably not without its effect; and if it was a proper one then to recommend the establishment of a constitution, it must be a proper one now to assist in its interpretation.

About the Author

Joe Wolverton will not allow anyone in his house who doesn't know the lyrics to "Hey, Porter," "Johnny Reb," and "A Country Boy Can Survive." He's a man of exacting standards in a world without any.

When he's not holding his guests lyrically liable, Joe lives to share timeless principles of liberty with his readers and to help them use their new knowledge in becoming friends of freedom and defenders of the Constitution.

After earning a bachelor's degree in Political Science, Joe returned home to Memphis, Tennessee to attend law school. He earned his Juris Doctorate in 2001 and then practiced law as a constitutional attorney in Memphis, Nashville, and Chattanooga until 2009.

In 2004, Joe began writing for *The New American* magazine and since then he has traveled around the country sharing the truth about the role of individual responsibility and morality in maintaining liberty. His articles appear regularly in numerous national and international publications.

He is the author of *The Real James Madison*, the first Madison biography in decades to contain the complete text of Madison's rarely mentioned republican essays. Later this year Joe will release a groundbreaking book revealing, for the first time in over a century, selections from the 37 books most influential on the Founding Fathers, books that have been scrubbed from our cultural memory.

Joe will someday soon move back home to the South and settle with his family on a farm where the only way you'll ever find him is if he wants you to.

AVAILABLE FROM SHOTWELL PUBLISHING

If you enjoyed this book, perhaps some of our other titles will pique your interest. The following titles are now available for your reading pleasure... Enjoy!

Joyce Bennett

Maryland, My Maryland: The Cultural Cleansing of a Small Southern State

Jerry Brewer

Dismantling the Republic

Andrew P. Calhoun, Jr.

My Own Darling Wife: Letters From a Confederate Volunteer [John Francis Calhoun]

John Chodes

Segregation: Federal Policy or Racism?

Washington's KKK: The Union League During Southern Reconstruction

Paul C. Graham

Confederaphobia: An American Epidemic

When the Yankees Come: Former South Carolina Slaves Remember Sherman's Invasion

Joseph Jay

Sacred Conviction: The South's Stand for Biblical Authority

Suzanne Parfitt Johnson

Maxcy Gregg's Sporting Journals 1842 - 1858

James R. Kennedy

Dixie Rising: Rules for Rebels

James R. & Walter D. Kennedy

Punished with Poverty: The Suffering South

Yankee Empire: Aggressive Abroad and Despotic At Home

Philip Leigh

The Devil's Town: Hot Spring During the Gangster Era

U.S. Grant's Failed Presidency

Michael Martin

Southern Grit: Sensing the Siege at Petersburg

Lewis Liberman

Snowflake Buddies: ABCs for Leftism for Kids!

Charles T. Pace

Lincoln As He Was

Southern Independence. Why War?

James Rutledge Roesch

From Founding Fathers to Fire Eaters: The Constitutional Doctrine of States' Rights in the Old South

Kirkpatrick Sale

*Emancipation Hell: The
Tragedy Wrought By Lincoln's
Emancipation Proclamation*

Karen Stokes

*A Legion of Devils: Sherman
in South Carolina*

Carolina Love Letters

John Vinson

Southerner, Take Your Stand!

Howard Ray White

Understanding Creation and Evolution

Walter Kirk Wood

*Beyond Slavery: The Northern
Romantic Nationalist Origins
of America's Civil War*

Clyde N. Wilson

*Annals of the Stupid Party: Republicans
Before Trump (The Wilson Files 3)*

*Lies My Teacher Told Me: The
True History of the War for
Southern Independence*

*Nullification: Reclaiming Consent of
the Governed (The Wilson Files 2)*

*The Old South: 50 Essential Books
(Southern Reader's Guide I)*

*The War Between the States:
60 Essential Books (Southern
Reader's Guide II)*

*The Yankee Problem: An American
Dilemma (The Wilson Files 1)*

———————————

GREEN ALTAR BOOKS

(Literary Imprint)

Randall Ivey

*A New England Romance &
Other SOUTHERN Stories*

James Everett Kibler

Tiller (Clay Bank County, IV)

Karen Stokes

Belles: A Carolina Romance

Honor in the Dust

The Immortals

*The Soldier's Ghost: A
Tale of Charleston*

———————————

GOLD-BUG

(Mystery & Suspense Imprint)

Michael Andrew Grissom

Billie Jo

Brandi Perry

Splintered: A New Orleans Tale

Martin L. Wilson

To Jekyll and Hide

Free Book Offer

Sign-up for new release notifications and receive a **FREE** downloadable edition of *Lies My Teacher Told Me: The True History of the War for Southern Independence* by Dr. Clyde N. Wilson by visiting FreeLiesBook.com or by texting the word "Dixie" to 345345. You can always unsubscribe and keep the book, so you've got nothing to lose!

Made in the USA
Las Vegas, NV
22 March 2023

69499399R00100